I Am...

I Am...

MARISSA ALFANO

Cover Design by Murphy Rae, www.murphyrae.com
Photography by Victoria Batkiewicz
Edited by Ink Deep Editing
Formatting by Allusion Publishing, www.allusionpublishing.com

ISBN: 979-8-9898149-1-6

@IAmByMarissaAlfano
@MarissaAlfano
info@iambymarissaalfano.com
www.MarissaAlfano.com

For the girl who wanted to be loved by a man
that could never love her the way she deserved.

For the girl who lost herself in the relationship or marriage.

For the girl who finally chooses herself and her healing.

For the girl who realizes she has and always will be enough.

Table of Contents

Playlist

Part 1: My Story

Truth About You–Mitchell Tenpenny

Thru Your Phone–Cardi B

Best Thing I Never Had–Beyonce

Bed of Lies–Nicki Minaj

Vampire-Olivia Rodrigo

What He Didn't Do-Carly Pearce

I Hope–Gabby Barrett

Narcissist–Lauren Spencer Smith

You Should Be Sad-Halsey

Mountain With A View-Kelsea Ballerini

On Purpose (For My Future Daughter)–Bellah Mae

Interlude (Full Length)–Kelsea Ballerini

Mine-Kelly Clarkson

Part 2: My Healing

Karma (Taylor's Version)–Taylor Swift

It's Been a Year–Ashley Cooke

Rise Up-Andra Day

What I Have–Kelsea Ballerini

Vigilante Shit–Taylor Swift

Call Your Sister-Taylor Edwards

All I Know So Far–P!nk

Fight Song-Rachel Platten

Pick Me Up-Gabby Barrett

Universe–Kelsea Ballerini

Your Bones-Chelsea Cutler

Leave Me Again-Kelsea Ballerini

She Got Her Own–Ne-Yo, Jamie Foxx, Fabulous

I Am Woman–Emmy Meli

God Is a Woman–Ariana Grande

The Good Ones–Gabby Barrett

Introduction

A COUPLE OF years back, it dawned on me that it's not that big of a world after all. Everyone is fighting their own battles and doing their best. This book started as a journal to help me heal, but then I realized that sharing my story could help someone else. I thought to myself that if someone read this and felt less alone on their journey, or felt inspired to embark on their own healing journey and quite possibly make the greatest comeback of all time, then I would have accomplished what I set out to do.

In Part 1, I tell my story of the last ten years. The all-encompassing, over-the-moon love story. The fairy-tale life. The deceit and lies that brought me to my knees. The way I lost myself in fighting the not-so-good fight for my marriage. The start of my healing in therapy. The end of my marriage. How I embarked on a spiritual healing journey.

In Part 2, I share the lessons and knowledge I gained while on my healing journey and the ways you can apply them to your life. The work I've done to heal has been the hardest work I've ever done, but it has transformed my life, and it can transform yours too. My healing journey has led me to the beautiful, peaceful, and fulfilling place I am now. You deserve to be here too, so let's get there together!

Before you dive in, I want to thank you for being here. Thank you for letting me share my journey with you. I believe connection is such a beautiful privilege, and it's an honor to share this space with you. Thank you!

Part 1

My Story

Chapter 1

I Am in Love

I RECENTLY SAW a mutual friend of Parker's and mine, and she asked what had happened between us. Before I could share, she said, "Parker was in love with you ever since we were young" and for a moment it brought me back to much simpler times. Days that were woven with hand-holding, kisses on the front porch of my parents' house, and AIM messages back and forth. Those days and nights felt like they'd last forever. I wish that version of Parker was the one left in my memory instead of the one that is.

Parker and I grew up together. Our parents live on the same block. We were both part of a group of neighborhood kids that hung out all the time. There were after-school meetups and summers spent playing manhunt, swimming in the pool, and exploring the neighborhood. Parker always had a crush on me, and I always thought he was cute. He'd sit next to me if we were watching a scary movie, and we'd secretly hold hands, thinking no one would notice. One night when we were about thirteen years old, I was eating dinner with my best friend and my sister at my parents' dining room table, and Parker unexpectedly knocked on the front door. He asked if the girls and I wanted to hang out. I told him we were eating and we'd be out afterwards. He smiled, leaned in, and kissed me. My first kiss! I walked back inside with pink cheeks, feeling a rush of excitement. We scarfed down the rest of our food and ran out the door to go meet up with "the boy who kissed me" and all our other friends. We were just in time to play manhunt in the dark, where Parker and I would sneak another kiss or two.

Those summer days felt like they would go on forever, but before long Halloween rolled around, and it was too cold to hang outside. In the winter, we only saw each other in school, but before we knew it, it was April again and the neighborhood kids were reunited! The summer before I started high school, I started hanging out with a different group of friends. Sadly, that was the end of our neighborhood group. We were growing up and our lives were going in different directions. I always used to think about Noah and Allie from the *Notebook* when I thought of Parker and me. Although we were young, I truly believed it was true love and, like them, we'd reconnect later in life.

After many years apart, our paths brought us back together, and that young love was relit. Superstorm Sandy hit Long Island on October 29, 2012, when I was home from college. Parker messaged me on Facebook to see how my family was doing. Parker and I were in very similar places in life, and it felt like we had the world at our fingertips. Both of us were fresh out of long-term relationships and had just graduated from college and started our careers. From October 2012 until September 2013, I was single and out partying with my friends and dancing the nights away. Parker would always come meet me out, keep an eye on me, and make sure I got home safe. He asked to take me on a date more times than I could count during those eleven months, but I always had an excuse. I didn't want to be tied down again, but the single life got old quickly, and Parker was right there waiting when it did.

I went on a family vacation to Aruba in July of 2013, and there was no Wi-Fi on the beach back then. You only had Wi-Fi in your hotel room. I remember sitting on the beach and missing Parker. I sent him a Facebook message to let him know I was thinking of him. After I got home from that trip, we were inseparable. It was the beginning of a beautiful love story. I had met my perfect match, and he was falling for me just as quickly as I was for him. On September 8, 2013,

Parker asked me to drive down to the beach with him. We cuddled up on a blanket underneath the most gorgeous sunset. The sky was painted blue, orange, and pink for us. I was safe there in his arms. It felt like the rest of the world disappeared. He tucked my hair behind my ear as my head lay on his chest, and he asked me to be his girlfriend. I remember it as a very easy yes, but he claims I said no, then said yes. The moon sat perfectly above the sunset, and I remember thinking this was the start of something great.

With each passing day, we fell deeper and deeper in love. We lived separately at our parents' homes so we could save money for our dream house. Every waking moment that we were not working, we spent together. We couldn't get enough of one another. On the weekends we went together to car shows, ran errands, went on dates, picked pumpkins, went out with friends, and spent time with family. We connected on many levels. We both wanted to be successful, travel, and own a beautiful home, so that's what we worked towards every day.

During one of our deeper conversations, Parker shared that he didn't believe in cheating or divorce. I agreed that I didn't believe in cheating, but I did believe in divorce. It seems strange because my parents have been married for thirty-eight years, but I always felt like people must choose to be in a marriage and if at any point you no longer chose the marriage, you must get out of it. Parker also shared that he wanted children. I didn't know if I wanted to have kids, but I knew that if we got married, it was something I'd honor for him. This was also strange because I love children. It was like my subconscious was seeing something I wasn't, and it was already sending up a warning signal.

In July of 2014, Parker came on our annual family trip to Aruba, and I introduced him to my favorite place on earth. My parents traveled there on their honeymoon in 1987, and this island held a special place in all of our hearts. He loved it just as much as I did. He fit right in with my family. I told him that since I was a little girl, I had told my dad that I wanted to get married in Aruba. Parker was a planner and a thinker, so he had to let a destination wedding marinate in his mind. But one of the most wonderful things about Parker was that he never said no. Even when I had crazy dreams and ideas, he would listen, not say much, and then figure out a way to make it a reality. I loved him for that.

The following year we did a lot of traveling. We went to Florida for my best friend's engagement party and to visit Parker's grandparents. We went back to Aruba and somehow found ourselves looking at engagement rings. I knew I wanted an oval diamond, and Parker had done his research on clarity, color, and cut. I have to say I was impressed. We ended up finding a beautiful oval diamond and a setting that had more diamonds than I knew what to do with. I felt like I was dreaming. My dream man, my dream ring, my dream vacation. I never wanted to wake up. After Aruba, we went to Texas with two of Parker's best guy friends. It was supposed to be a boys trip, but I was like one of the boys, so they let me tag along. I left that trip feeling like I knew exactly why Parker loved Isaac and Tanner so much, and I loved them too. We finished the year in Ocean City, Maryland, for one of Parker's beloved car shows. Parker adored cars. It was a passion of his, and it was only right that one requirement for our future home was a two-car garage. I remember Parker's mom saying to me, "You'll always know where Parker is. He won't be out at the bar drinking and fooling around. He'll be in the garage working on his cars." I could easily envision that in our future, and I couldn't wait to live together one day!

My favorite year together was 2016. In January, we celebrated my twenty-fifth birthday. Parker decorated my bedroom with dozens of red and pink roses, big pink balloons that said twenty-five, and a gorgeous pair of red-bottomed Louboutin heels. His gifts and his love were over the top and extravagant. They would make any girl feel on top of the world. In February, we flew to Las Vegas to celebrate Valentine's Day. When we checked into the hotel, we upgraded to a suite that had floor-to-ceiling windows. Parker stood at the window looking down at the Las Vegas Strip and said, "We made it!"

When we weren't traveling, Parker was on the hunt for our dream house. He would spend hours looking on Zillow. He'd turn the computer towards me and say, "What do you think of this?" and when we were at work, he would send me links to houses every couple of hours. I would watch Parker calculate every expense down to the cent to see what we could afford. I could stare at him with that calculator all day. When he was passionate about something, he would put so much time and energy into it. He would light up when he talked about it. I knew it was only a matter of time until he found the perfect house for us.

Falling for Parker was effortless. It felt like I'd hit a grand slam with this man. The romance, the fancy dinners, the expensive gifts, the flowers, the passion, I could go on and on. One vacation topped the next. He quite literally swept me off my feet.

Looking back now, I can see that the extravagant gifts and trips were a red flag. Especially in our early twenties. But they sure as hell were the perfect disguise for what was missing inside of Parker and what I would soon uncover.

Chapter 2

I Am Ignoring the Red Flags

YOU KNOW THE meme that says, I saw the red flags and thought I was at a carnival? Well, long story short, I was at a carnival wearing the rose-colored glasses that I won at the balloon dart game for eight glorious years. I wish I was kidding.

When Parker and I first started dating, we meshed friend groups, and we would all hang out and go out every weekend together. Parker dated a girl named Melanie in high school and in college off and on. I knew Melanie because she dated another one of my guy friends when we were in high school. Melanie was always very nice to me, and she was coming around the friend group more often because she was newly dating our friend Travis. As time went on, Travis, Melanie, Parker, and I started hanging out all the time. We'd go on double dates and out partying. I knew Parker and Melanie had dated way back when, but I didn't think too much of it. Melanie and I were getting closer, and I considered her a good friend. We would hang out without the guys too as we were building our friendship.

One day, Melanie came over to my house with her son, and it was like any other girl's night in. We were sitting on my bed catching up while I was playing with her son. Further into the conversation, she randomly said, "About six months ago, I was hooking up with this guy and I asked myself if I loved him, and I just really didn't know."

I was confused about why she would bring up this past guy out of the blue when she'd been dating Travis for a while now. It didn't make sense. I responded, "Who is the guy?"

Melanie said with a shaky voice, "Uh, I don't know. You don't know him."

I watched her body language as she sat on my bed and lied straight to my face. At that moment, I knew she was talking about Parker. Parker and I had been dating for six months at this point, so naturally my stomach turned. Melanie could see it clicking in my head. It took me a minute to silently put the pieces together, but I did. Cue the awkward silence. Then I felt myself getting angry. *How dare she come to my house, sit on my bed, and so casually drop this bomb on me.* I said, "I think it's time for you to leave." Melanie nodded her head in agreement, grabbed her son's bag and toys, and left my house. I didn't even say anything to her as she left because there wasn't much to be said. Now I can see that she was warning me, but at that time, I thought she was intentionally stirring the pot and trying to hurt me.

I sat on my bed for a few minutes in silence, trying to understand what Melanie had just told me. Parker had been pursuing me for a year and a half now, but we had only been dating for six months, so it wasn't technically cheating. *But what the fuck.* If Parker and Melanie had been fucking right up until he asked me to be his girlfriend, I would have really appreciated a heads-up from somebody. Instead, I befriended Melanie like we were going to be lifelong friends while she and Parker made dreamy eyes at each other while I was playing with her son. It made me sick.

I got myself together and, as cool as a cucumber, I called Parker and asked him to come over to hang out. Parker made his way over and got into my bed like any other night. I cuddled up next to him, ready to shoot off some burning questions. I asked him when he and Melanie had last hooked up and he confidently said, "Years ago in college." I told him that Melanie had said that they were hooking up six months before and had been falling in love.

That was the first time I saw Parker's soul leave his body. When Parker lies, his skin becomes almost see-through. It turns a shade of milky yellow, and you can see the veins in his face. I wish I could say this was the only time I'd see that face, but it wasn't. His voice shook when he said, "It wasn't six months ago. Actually... I don't know. Maybe it was. I'm not sure. Yeah, I'm not sure." I stared at Parker with a puzzled look on my face. *Was it normal for people to lie to your face? People that you love?* I didn't think so, but it had happened twice in one night, and I was starting to feel crazy.

I said, "I think you should go," and Parker said, "No, Marissa. We need to talk about this. I don't know why I didn't tell you. It was before me and you." I told him I wanted him to leave. He begged to stay and for forgiveness, but he ultimately ended up leaving. I curled up in my bed alone and cried. I felt like a fucking idiot. Everyone had known this but me. No, it wasn't cheating because we weren't technically together, but all three of them knew this secret. It was a big secret. I couldn't understand how none of them felt like it might be a good idea to tell me. If I was fucking someone right up until Parker asked me to be his girlfriend, I sure as hell wouldn't allow Parker and that guy to be friends, let alone good friends. It was weird. It was so fucking weird.

Parker texted me when he got home. "I know you wanted me to leave, but I didn't want to leave. I never meant for this to happen. I never meant to hurt you. I've completely fallen for you, and I've never felt this way about anyone else in my life. I would never risk losing this relationship or you. You have to believe that, Marissa. She meant nothing to me. I know you aren't going to believe me now, but it's the truth. I will keep telling you how much you mean to me every single day until you believe me. There is no one for me but you. I'm sorry."

I read the messages and didn't respond.

"Please respond to me, Marissa. I'm so sorry."

I buried my head in my pillow and cried myself to sleep. In the morning, he texted and called a few times, but I needed some space.

The whole situation felt gross. I told my mom and sister about what had happened, and my mom said, "People make mistakes, Mariss. Give him a call back." Later that afternoon, I called Parker back, and he said, "I didn't know how to tell you. You don't normally have to tell your new girl about your old girl, but then Travis started dating her and now we are here and I'm so sorry."

I said, "The only thing I ask for is honesty. I respect honesty. I don't care how bad the information will hurt me, just be honest." Parker apologized again.

So, yes, I was at the 'Ignoring Red Flags' carnival. The flags were waving everywhere, the games were all lit up, the music was loud, the Ferris wheel was going round and round, and somehow Parker pulled me right back in.

One of the few times I went to Parker's parents' house, we walked into his bedroom, and he quite literally leaped over to his desk and shoved something in the top drawer. I made a mental note and got into his bed. I knew it was only a matter of time before he would have to go to the bathroom. When he did, I made my way over to his desk and opened the drawer. I found a vape and all the gadgets that go with it. I'm not a smoker and had made it clear to Parker early on in our relationship that I didn't do drugs and I didn't want to be with someone who did drugs or smoked. Whether that was cigarettes or a vape, it didn't align with me, and it was non-negotiable. He agreed and said he also didn't want the person he was dating to be a smoker or into drugs.

When he got back from the bathroom, I was sitting at his desk with the vape and all the accessories on his desk in front of me. "Did you forget to tell me something?" I asked.

"It's not drugs, and I knew you'd get mad," he replied.

What a great response. Hell yes, I was mad. Why was he lying again? He'd had the same view on smoking and vaping as me just a few months before, but that seemed to slip his mind now. Bravo, Parker. I said, "Just stop lying to me. It's not that fucking hard. If you're into smoking, tell me. Just be honest with me. All I ask is that you be honest with me." I crawled back into his bed. As we lay there together watching MTV, a commercial with a girl lying in a hospital bed with a hole in her neck from vaping came on. We both started laughing. The truth was that was exactly how I didn't want my life to turn out. I didn't want to be with someone who smoked or someone who lied. This was a small lie in the grand scheme of things. Parker promised to stop vaping.

It wasn't long after the Melanie drama that Parker had his eyes on someone else and, unfortunately, that person wasn't me. Allow me to introduce you to Allison, someone I, unfortunately, will never forget for the rest of my life. Allison and Parker worked together at a law firm that Allison's dad owned. Parker had invited me to his work event in New York City, which was just a few blocks from my job, and I was able to go meet all his colleagues. I got to the restaurant, and Parker was waiting for me outside the front doors. I remember thinking how handsome he looked. We didn't get ready for work together, so seeing him in a button-down, slacks and a nice pair of shoes really did it for me. He pulled me in close and kissed me like he had missed me all day. Shortly after arriving, Parker introduced me to Allison. The way she greeted me and her body language towards me felt wildly ungenuine. From the second I met her, my body quite literally repelled her energy. I watched her dance around the room from one group of people to the next, begging for attention. Her voice, laugh, and comments were loud and exaggerated because she wanted all eyes in the room on her. We all know someone who naturally attracts everyone's attention without doing a single thing. It's like their energy and being are vibrating at the highest frequency, and they are a magnet for everyone else in the room. Allison was clearly screaming out to be that girl. It's just not in the cards for some people.

Later in the evening, Parker and I were standing in a circle of his colleagues. I was a few people over from Parker and was chatting with the people next to me. I saw Allison pop up right in between

Parker and the person he was standing next to, and I didn't think much of it. But then, to my disbelief, I saw her caressing his arm and rubbing up on the side of his body, and he seemed unfazed. Was I seeing this correctly? Why was he so unbothered? It seemed like that was a normal occurrence for them by the way they both were acting so natural. Why would they be acting like this right in front of me? I would never let a male coworker touch me like that.

I took a deep breath and walked away towards the bathroom in a fury. I closed and locked the bathroom stall door. I texted my sister, feeling sick to my stomach. My sister said I had to confront him because this behavior was not normal or acceptable. She was right. I felt so dirty having seen them act like that. After a few minutes, I gathered myself and my thoughts, and I walked out. Parker was waiting for me right outside of the bathroom and he said, "Is everything okay?" *What the fuck do you think? Did you think I was shitting in there? No, I wish that was the case. Instead, I'm texting my sister about the stupid shit you're doing right in front of my face.* I said, "I think it's time to go." He asked me what was wrong, but I didn't say anything. I was fuming inside. Absolutely furious. We grabbed our jackets and headed out of the restaurant. On our walk to Penn Station, I said, "You and Allison seem very comfortable with one another. She was caressing your arm." Parker replied with his world renowned, go-to response, "You're crazy. She's my boss's daughter." I was so fucking mad. No coworkers touch each other like that unless something is going on. He swore up and down that nothing was happening with Allison and I was overreacting. We fought the entire train ride home.

Here I was again at the carnival, with Parker convincing me that the caressing never happened. I started to question if I was crazy. It was slowly transforming from a carnival to a circus. Cue the circus animals.

Parker played in a hockey league with some guys from his job, and Allison was the unofficial team cheerleader. Allison's fiancé,

Josh, was on the team too. I would occasionally go to watch Parker play. For the record, I don't hate people. I have a lot of patience, and I give everyone the benefit of the doubt. That part of me was non-existent when Allison was around. My body knew that her energy was not good. She made my skin crawl, and I couldn't even pretend to like her. I had never felt this way about anyone else in my life.

It all makes sense looking back, but at the time I just knew that I felt incredibly turned off by Allison. Seeing them together made my stomach turn. I couldn't stand sitting near her at the hockey games or even listening to her voice. She would tell me the funny things that Parker did at work to make her laugh. She loved that she was a part of his work life and that I wasn't. It's hard to explain but she made it so obvious. I fucking hated the way she made me feel. I hated how Parker kept putting me in these uncomfortable situations. I'd never do that to him.

One night, Parker fell asleep before me, which was a rare occurrence, and I knew this was my opportunity to look through his phone. I went right to the text exchange between him and Allison. Allison said, "I don't think your girlfriend likes me" and Parker replied, "She doesn't like you lol." I don't know what I expected to see, but it sure as hell wasn't that. Parker didn't even try to cover up. He was sharing things with Allison that he really shouldn't be. *Why were they even talking about me?* It didn't feel like this was the first time my name had been brought up. Something didn't feel right, and I couldn't shake it.

When I confronted him in the morning, he said, "Well, I wasn't going to lie. You don't like her." *What does he mean that he wasn't going to lie? He lies to me on the regular. He can't lie to her? I have valid reasons to not like her. She can't keep her hands to herself, and my boyfriend doesn't know right from wrong.*

"You lie to me all the time, how come you can't lie to her?" I said. I knew exactly what he was going to say before he even said it—you're crazy.

"You're blowing this out of proportion and acting crazy," he replied. "You don't like her. It's not a secret. It's not weird that she said that to me."

"I think it's weird that I'm being brought up in your conversation to begin with. She feels comfortable enough to express something about your girlfriend. Nonetheless, I don't like her. You guys are colleagues, not close friends. Why does it matter if I like her or not? Why am I being brought up?"

He said, "She's my boss's daughter. When she talks to me at work, I respond. When she texts me, I respond. There's nothing more to it. You are making something out of nothing."

Maybe I was making something out of nothing. I just couldn't stand how she made me feel. She made me question my relationship. She made me question Parker's commitment to me. In a weird way, it felt like we were competing for Parker, and I fucking hated it.

I can see now that I was wrapped in a web of thinking this was the big love I had always dreamed of, and I let him convince me that his actions were harmless. When he'd call me crazy, I'd start to question myself. He somehow always convinced me to believe him and this, my friends, is textbook gaslighting.

Chapter 3

I Am Engaged

JUNE 25, 2016, started out like any other day. Parker was working. I was lying in my parents' backyard with my sister, taking in the sun. She asked if I wanted to grab lunch with her and her husband Kraig. I put a dress on over my bathing suit and the three of us headed to the Cheesecake Factory. When we arrived back at my parents' house, there was a small table on their front porch with a dozen roses. I looked at my sister and said, "Did you forget your anniversary?" and she said, "No, did you?" I said, "No, it's not mine." Puzzled, I walked up to the front porch and saw that the card said Marissa. My hands began to tremble, and my heart began to race.

The card read:

"Babe, since the day that I met you, you have been the most perfect and amazing thing in my life. You are one of the most beautiful, caring, and thoughtful people anyone could ask for. You have been the perfect girl to me and have given me anything I could ask for. I just wanted to tell you that I love you and it's my turn to return the favor and give you something you have been waiting for. At this point, you are standing at your door, wondering what is going on. I want to make today the most special day of your life and not just have myself but everyone else who means so much to us. I need you to get ready, wear your favorite dress, shoes, and makeup because today is the day I show you how much I love you. I have many exciting things planned that are important to us, important times and places in our relationship. The real question is can you remember what they are?

Clue #1: Where is the place where I first said, "I love you"? I need you to drive to the place where I first said I love you. Your next clue will be waiting at that location. Good luck! I love you and you're one step closer. I can't wait to see you. Love, Parker.

P.S. Your sister is going to be with you throughout this whole process. Let her take pictures/videos. You will thank us later. Even though you should remember the answers to my questions, if you don't, she has the answers. <3"

As tears streamed down my face, I turned to my sister and said, "Is this real?" and she said, "Yes, let's get ready!" This was a day I'd waited for my entire life. I couldn't believe it. I rushed into my bedroom and put on a brand-new dress I hadn't even tried on yet. Like magic, it fit perfectly.

Parker told me he loved me for the first time at the Emporium in Patchogue while we were celebrating my twenty-third birthday. So that's where my sister drove me to. On our way there, I had a million questions for her, but she was not giving away any answers or further clues. She liked seeing me squirm. I like to be in control and have everything planned out, so I was very much out of my element. We arrived at the Emporium, and I could see Parker's two best friends, Tanner and Isaac, waiting there for me. We parked the car, and I jumped out. Tanner and Isaac each gave me a dozen roses, making me laugh. I needed it. I felt like I had been crying happy tears for hours now. Shortly after, Isaac handed me the second clue. Cue the tears again.

The card read:

"Marissa, there is not a day that goes by that I do not think about you. You are my everything and my world. I am so grateful to have someone so supportive in my life. You are one of the most hardworking people that I have ever seen, and I admire that in you. Everything from your smile to your laugh to when you get angry. I love everything about you, and I love everything about us. I have never been so happy before in my life, and you being in my life makes me so happy. There is not a day that I can remember that I haven't looked forward to getting home and spending time with you. At this point, I can't wait to spend the rest of our lives together! I wanted to choose important locations to us and share them with important people in our lives. As you know, Tanner and Isaac are both very important people in my life, and I look at them like my brothers. I am beyond happy that you get along with them and they love you just as much as I do. The fact that you can hang out with us when it's just the guys proves to me that you are so easygoing and lovable. I have chosen them with this location because Emporium is the location where I first said I love you and where I fell in love with you. I want Tanner's and Isaac's goofiness and funniness to really brighten up this perfect day for you. We are going to have so much fun in our relationship and this was a perfect example of how I wanted to express that to you.

Clue #2: Where was the location as a child, you, I, and Marc spent most of our time?"

Marc was part of the neighborhood group, and he also had a crush on me when we were younger. Parker and Marc would fight over who was going to save me during the lifeguard game in the pool. Parker always won.

We spent all our summers at my parents' house, so this clue was easy. My sister and I got back in her car and headed back home. When we came through the front door, the house was quiet, but I could see everyone on the back deck. We went outside and there was my mom, dad, brother, grandma, and Kraig. Each of them had a dozen roses for me. I had more roses than I knew what to do with. Parker had set up a beautiful table with framed photos of us. I put the eighty-four roses I had received that day on the table too. I sat down at the table with my family, and we talked about what an incredible day this was. I remember my dad saying, "We are so excited to have Parker join our family, Mariss." I couldn't stop crying. I imagine that when one of your children, especially a daughter, finds someone that she wants to spend her life with, as a dad, you want the absolute best for her. You want someone that would plan a five-hour proposal with hundreds of roses and a well-thought-out plan. You'd want your daughter to feel like she was the only girl in the world and to be treated like a queen. That's exactly how I felt that day. The world stopped moving, and my dreams were coming true. After about an hour, my dad handed me the third clue.

The card read:

"You are the most important thing in my life. You are so beautiful, caring, and intelligent. I love how we are with each other and how we both want the same thing in life. I can't wait to see what our future looks like and am so excited to see how we are. I can't wait to travel the world with you and do so many fun activities. I love spending all my time with you as much as possible and would not change that for the world. You make me so proud of the things you achieve and the hardworking attitude you have. You are going to be the perfect wife. You check all the requirements that I want in a woman, and I am so happy that we started talking again, which was able to lead us to this moment. We turned a hurricane disaster into one of the most important dates of our lives. The location with your family is an obvious one. Family is one of the most important things in our lives. We come from different types of families. In the end, we both love our families and the way they brought us up. I am so honored to call your family mine and be able to celebrate everything with each other. Your parents have been my second family for the past three years, and I am so happy they brought up such a beautiful, strong girl. Your mother, father, brother, sister, and brother-in-law are going to be such a huge part of our lives, and I wanted them to be part of this special day. Love, Parker."

Clue #3: Where is the location we spend all our anniversaries, date nights, and special dinners with each other?

Our favorite date night spot was an Italian restaurant in our hometown, Verace. Vick and I got back in the car and made our way there. As we walked in, I could see Parker's parents sitting at a table with huge smiles on their faces. Vick and I sat down with them, and I was so happy to see them. The waitress asked if I wanted a drink and without any hesitation, I said, "Wine. I need some wine." We all laughed. I needed it to take the edge off, as I had been crying happy tears for hours now! Parker's mom shared stories about when she and Parker's dad first met and how he asked her to be his girlfriend. It was sweet. She then told us how he proposed and how the rest was history. It was such a special moment to share with them. I drank a glass of wine in three minutes flat. I'm sure Parker's mom was hoping her future daughter-in-law was not an alcoholic. After about an hour, Parker's mom handed me the fourth clue.

The card read:

"Marissa, my soulmate, wife, other half, my rock, and my world. Those are just some of the words that come to mind when I think of you. There isn't anything in this world I would not do for you. We always say that we are each other in different forms. I truly believe that. Our personalities are identical, and we think exactly alike. I would rather have someone who understands my craziness and goofiness than someone who is the total opposite. Since the day that we met, I have been crazy in love with you. I can say at three years I am just as in love with you as I was on day one. There isn't anyone in the world who I've met that I did not want to brag to about how amazing my girlfriend is. I cannot wait to see what the future holds for us and how strong we are going to grow as a couple. I've been wanting to do this for quite some time now. I really needed time to plan how I was going to express the love I have for someone who I would give anything for. Verace has been one of our favorite spots to go on dates together because it's so easy, fancy, and you get to dress up and look beautiful like you always do. I have chosen my parents to represent this location because, even though my parents don't go out on dates and to the movies a lot, they still love each other just as much when they sit home as they do when they go out. Even though I love going out to fancy places with you and getting dressed up, I do love spending nights in, cuddling and watching movies, equally the same. We have just as much fun going out as we do when we spend a night together."

Clue #4: Where is the location where it all started, and I asked you to be my girlfriend? (Even though you said no the first time, I still love you). Field 3, first entrance, and follow the sunset towards field 2.

Vick and I were off again! To the beach we go! As we drove over the Robert Moses Bridge to get to the beach, I stared out the window at a perfect sunset. I remember saying to myself, how could I be so lucky? My heart was so full, and he hadn't even proposed yet. As we got out of the car, my sister got her camera and GoPro ready, and we made our way down to the beach. We had to walk a long way to get to Parker, but he was one of the only people on the beach. As I got closer to him, I could see candles, rose petals, and a blanket. Parker was standing directly in the center of the blanket. I ran to him and kissed him as tears streamed down my face. He asked, "Have you been drinking wine?" and we both started laughing so hard. As our laughter faded, Parker looked deep into my eyes and smiled, then read my last clue. As he spoke the words he had written, there were tears falling down his face. I don't remember much of what he said, but I do remember thinking, *I'm so lucky that he chose me to marry him. I'm the luckiest girl in the world.*

He got down on one knee, took the ring out of his back pocket, looked up at me, and said "Marissa Renee, will you marry me?" and I said, "Yes. Of course, yes!" There was nothing I was more sure of. I loved Parker with every fiber of my being. He placed the most beautiful oval diamond ring on my ring finger. He stood up, kissed me, and pulled me in close. I said, "I'm your fiancée!" He smiled and said, "Yes, you are, my love."

We sat down on the blanket, and my body fit perfectly next to his. He held me so tight, tighter than ever before. We laughed and cried. My sister took pictures of us. I held my hand out, and we both stared at this beautiful ring. It was perfect. This was pure bliss. Parker said, "One more surprise," and I said, "I don't know If I can handle another one," and we laughed. He took out a custom ring box engraved with my soon-to-be new last name. He was smiling so big. He was so proud of this day and his proposal. I was too. It was magical and over the top, which was typical for Parker. He goes big or he goes home, that's for sure.

We took a few more pictures down by the water, and I felt like I was walking on clouds. Our bodies were flowing and dancing together as we skipped through the sand hand in hand. The camera flashed time and time again, but it truly was like the world had stopped for us. Parker looked at me and said, "Are you ready for your last surprise?" We walked through the sand back to the beach parking lot. I could see our friends and families standing side by side, holding a huge banner with my first name and my soon-to-be last name. Everyone had huge smiles on their faces. We kissed and hugged everyone and thanked them. My mom admired my engagement ring and said, "Marissa, this ring is stunning!" She shouted to Parker, "You did so good, my son! You really did."

Parker popped a bottle of champagne, filled everyone's glasses, and said, "Cheers to our engagement and my future wife. This is a day we will always remember. I want to thank you guys for helping me pull this off. I know it was not easy, but look at the smile on Marissa's face. It was worth it. Cheers!" I sipped my champagne and stared at Parker. I was in awe of this man. My soon-to-be husband. He always pulled out all the stops, so this elaborate proposal was no different.

In hindsight, while the over-the-top-proposal was epic, it was also an example of love bombing. I felt lucky to be chosen by Parker for all of the wrong reasons. I felt like he had finally chosen me over all of his other flings. I had finally won. Unfortunately, in time, I'd learn that this wasn't a fight I wanted to win. My big oval engagement ring couldn't stand in for the true love that I was so badly seeking but would never find within Parker.

Chapter 4

I Am Living a Dream

MY DREAM PROPOSAL. My dream ring. Someone needed to pinch me to wake me up. It felt like we were about to embark on this new chapter together, and everything seemed to be falling perfectly into place.

Ever since I was a little girl, I'd told my dad that I wanted to get married in Aruba. I would sit on the beach with him every year and watch these beautiful brides walk down the aisle to their husbands. I couldn't picture my wedding any other way. It was surreal that I'd found a man that I was so deeply in love with, and he loved Aruba just as much as I did. And he wanted to make my dream of getting married there come true.

We wrapped up summer by going to Aruba for the week of Labor Day and met with a wedding planner. We signed a contract to get married on August 25, 2018. That gave us two years to save for and plan our dream wedding.

Over the next few months, I worked on save-the-dates, invitations, flowers, arches, photographers, videographers, musicians, DJs, food menus, transportation, hotel rooms, dresses, suits... the list went on and on. Meanwhile, Parker searched for our dream home.

In July of 2017, we went to look at a house by the water, and we both really liked it. It needed work, which wasn't ideal, but it had great bones and the location was awesome. As we were driving away from that house, we saw there was an open house a few houses down on a brand-new build. I was tired and didn't want to stop, but Parker finally convinced me. Thank goodness he did because this was my dream house. We walked inside and before we'd even seen the whole house, I said to the real estate agent, "We want to put an offer in." They didn't have any other offers, and they accepted our offer the following day. This house was perfect. It was an open-concept new build, steps away from the water. Another pinch-me moment.

In September, we made our way back to Aruba to finalize plans for the wedding, and in October I started the search for my dream wedding dress. I'm very decisive, so I didn't want this to be a long, dragged-out process. My mom, sister, and I entered the bridal store, and the sales associate directed us to the areas that were within our price range. Before I even started looking through those dresses, I saw this beautiful floral draped-sleeve dress hanging on the back wall. Even though it was above our budget, I pulled the dress out and said, "I need to try this." The price was about $500 more so it wasn't outrageous. I put the dress on, and I was ready to stop shopping, but I tried on five other dresses to appease my mom and the sales associate. Then I put the first dress back on and said yes to the dress. It was equal parts romantic, delicate, and elegant. I felt like the most beautiful girl in the world in that dress, and I knew Parker and my dad would feel the same way.

In December, we closed on the house. Home at last with the love of my life. As we unpacked our boxes, hung photos on the walls, and started this new chapter together, I felt an overwhelming amount of gratitude. I was so in love with Parker, and now I get to wake up beside him every single day. I imagined that one day we would welcome our first child into this house and how it wouldn't always be so clean and neat, but it would always be filled with love.

Looking back now, I can see that Parker's and my relationship was filled with lots of beautiful, extravagant things, but I was mistaking these "things" for love. The destination wedding and the big, new house were the perfect way to keep my focus elsewhere while Parker was leading a double life.

Chapter 3

I Am Being Cheated On

A FEW WEEKS after moving into the house, things changed. I couldn't ignore the huge shift in Parker's personality, actions, and moods. I remember him asking me if he could start playing video games with his friend, and I said I didn't mind. One night a week turned into two then four then six, and I was going to bed alone every night. This wasn't what I imagined living together would be like. Parker was becoming increasingly more irritable and mean as the days went by. When I would ask him what was wrong, he'd say work sucked or someone at work was annoying that day. It felt like an excuse, though, like I was the one bothering him. It seemed he would do anything to be anywhere besides with me, whether that was playing video games, playing hockey, staying late at work, or working on his cars. To be honest, it felt fucking horrible. How had the man I loved so much change so quickly? When we were living separately, he would move mountains to spend time with me. He would do anything to see me smile and make me happy. I missed that Parker. It felt like Parker and I were ships in the night, passing one another by, and it was always a cold fucking night.

Looking back now, I can see that when we were living separately, it was easier for him to live a double life. He started to play video games all night to escape his current reality and send as many text messages as he wanted to while I was fast asleep. Now that we lived together, I knew when he left for work and when he got home. Before, he could lie to me and I would have no idea. He became more irritable with me because he was in love with someone else.

I'll never forget July 6, 2018. My stomach still turns when I think about it. That night, I went to dinner with one of my good friends, and she gifted me the most beautiful cutting board and salad bowl that was engraved with my soon-to-be new last name and our wedding date. I could not wait to get home and show Parker and put it in our kitchen! When I got home from dinner, Parker was on the couch. I'd had a few glasses of wine at dinner and, naturally, I went home and wanted to have sex with my fiancé. I remember feeling like he was disconnected and cold, but we were having sex, so I just brushed it off as me overthinking.

After we finished our little rendezvous on the couch, Parker got up to get a drink from the kitchen and set his phone down on the dining room table. Soon after, I walked towards the kitchen, and Parker made his way upstairs to change for a hockey game he was playing in at 11 p.m. that night. Within seconds of him being upstairs, he came running back down the stairs to grab his phone off the dining room table. When I say he ran, I mean this man flew down the stairs at lightning speed. In this moment, I subconsciously knew something was wrong. My body could feel it, but my mind wouldn't acknowledge it...yet. I got into bed and Parker kissed me goodbye. As I lay in bed, I could feel myself getting tired. As my eyes started to close, I heard a voice within myself say, "Get up. Go into the office. Check the Apple Watch." This voice didn't scare me. It was like a gentle warning and a warm push to do something that I needed to do. It was a weird moment because I was about to fall asleep, but intuitively I knew I had to get up and do what I was told. The next two minutes were truly an out-of-body experience. I watched myself get out of bed and walk into his office. I sat down at his computer and took a deep breath. I never touched his computer that night. His Apple Watch sat on the charger, and with two clicks my entire world fell apart. I lost my breath as I scrolled through his text messages with Allison that

28

I was never intended to see. My heart shattered on his office floor. I couldn't even cry. I was in pure shock and started to shake.

The text thread included a conversation about not being able to meet up before work that morning because Parker was running late, sexy selfies, "I love yous," compliments of Allison's ass, and coordinating a meet-up before hockey. He asked her "Are you giving up that ass?" and she replied, "Don't I always?" They talked about how I was going to be in Atlanta for work the following week, and they'd have uninterrupted time together, and how Parker needed to clean his truck because they made it dirty.

I immediately called my sister and said, "Parker is cheating on me, and I need you to get here now," and she did just that. While my sister was on her way over, I called Parker and said, "You have to come home." He asked why, and I said, "I just need you to come home," and he said, "But why?" I said "Parker, I'm not going to say it a third time," and he said he was on his way. My sister arrived at the house within five minutes, and she said, "I can't believe this, Marissa. This can't be real. You guys are getting married in a month." I asked her to take a video of all the texts on his Apple Watch because we needed the evidence.

The front door unlocked. Cue the see-through, milky yellow skin and purple veins on Parker's face.

"What's the matter?" Parker asked.

"Do you think I'm stupid?"

"With what?"

"Allison! Go ahead, tell me what's going on with Allison. Tell me what's going on with your boss's daughter."

"What do you mean what's going on with my boss's daughter?"

"Parker, I read all of the messages. You didn't delete them in time. Tell me what's going on with your boss's daughter."

"There's nothing going on with my boss's daughter."

"Tell me what the fuck's going on, Parker. Stop acting like a fucking pussy. Are you guys having a relationship?"

"No."

"Parker, the wedding is off. You can go be with Allison. I cannot believe you would do this to me."

Parker kept denying anything was wrong, saying he didn't know what messages I meant.

"Okay, you don't know what's there?" I yelled. "They are from today, so I don't know how you don't know what the fuck you said. You just lost everything you had. This house is going on the market tomorrow for this fucking ugly-ass bitch. I'm getting a lawyer in the morning, and I am out of here. First thing in the morning my shit will be gone. This wedding is over. Over. You can fucking marry this bitch. I don't give a shit. She's in a fucking committed relationship and so are you. You are disgusting. This is it for us. And you have nothing to say."

"I didn't do anything wrong to you, Marissa. I'm sorry."

"You didn't do anything wrong to me? Do I even know you? I sleep next to you every single night, and I have no idea who you are. And I swear to god, I was always so scared this was going to happen."

I told Parker to give me his cell phone, and he handed it over. Any messages with Allison had been deleted. I called her from Parker's phone as Parker asked, "Who are you calling?"

"Hey, Allison. It's Marissa. I just read through yours and Parker's text messages. Do you think it's appropriate to communicate like this with a man who is not your husband? You're married. Parker is about to be. What is wrong with you?"

"Um... I think we're both in a very similar situation. We're just constantly frustrated with life, and we're trying to figure our lives out and we lean on each other."

"Do you see a future with Parker?"

"I don't know. Like you said, I'm married."

"Well, that doesn't mean anything at this point, right? I have all the messages saved, and they will be shown to your husband and your father. I find this all unfathomable. I would never do this. I feel sorry that you are in a position where you feel like you need to do this. You need to take a hard look in the mirror. The karma you will reap from this will go on forever. And quite honestly, I hope it does."

"So, you're basically risking Parker's career?"

"You don't have to worry about that. I can't believe you were planning to attend our wedding. What is wrong with you?"

"You'll have to take this up with your husband."

I hung up the phone and turned to Parker.

"You're not even just letting me down. You're letting everyone down." I yelled, "For a fucking side piece. You just have no emotion. You're not even crying."

"I know I'm going to lose it all. It had nothing to do with you."

"It must be me. What is it? What is it, Parker? I want to know."

"It's not you. You haven't done anything wrong."

"Are you not in love with me?" I asked.

"I am absolutely in love with you. I do want to marry you. I had all intentions of marrying you."

"I don't know what to say. I don't know what to do. We put this home together. We are about to get married. We planned this beautiful wedding. For what? For some fake fucking love? That I think I have. That we don't have. How could I be so foolish? I should have known from the fucking get-go when you were fucking Melanie that this wasn't going to work. People don't change, Parker." I paused. "Does Isaac know?"

"No, no one knows. I'm sorry."

"I don't feel it, Parker."

"I know, but I don't know what else to say. I'm sorry. It's not what I meant to happen.

"It's not what you meant to happen? What did you mean to happen?"

"I don't know. I don't know why I was doing it. I can't even give you a real reason why I was doing it."

"All I know is that I wake up at 4:45 every single morning so that we can have this beautiful life together. This beautiful fucking wedding. For what?" I asked. "I don't want it. I would rather live in a fucking hole with someone who adores me than do this. I would give all of this back to have someone who actually loves me. I don't want to be in this type of relationship."

"You don't have to do it. I understand. If you don't want to do it then we don't have to do it."

"Do what?"

"Be with me."

"Why is it so easy for you to say that? You're ready to pack your shit and go to Allison's house. So what do we do? What do we do with this wedding that eighty-five people are coming to? Do you have any feelings in your body? What are you feeling right now?"

"Numb."

"Why didn't you just say, 'I don't want to be with you'?"

"It's not that I don't want to be with you. I'm sorry. I'm seriously sorry. I'll say it over and over again. It didn't mean anything."

"I can't believe you would do this. How do we even come back from this? What do we even do?"

"I wish I had the answers, Mariss. I truly understand why you don't want to be with me."

"And you're just ready to let it go like that?"

"I'm not ready to let it go, but it's your decision. I fucked up. I'll show you that it didn't mean anything. I still love you. I still want to be with you. Everything was true with you. It's not like it was a lie. It had nothing to do with you."

"You're supposed to be my ride or die. You're supposed to be my husband. You're supposed to be my partner. I don't know what I did to deserve this. Maybe we're not supposed to be together, Parker. Maybe this isn't it. Do you ever feel that way?"

"No."

"Maybe this is a sign that we aren't supposed to get married. There's going to be someone else out there that it'll be better with, and this will never happen. Cause I cannot believe that God would let me marry someone who would do this to me. I think I do too much good to let this happen to me. You, on the other hand, I don't know. I don't know what's in store for you, but I give everything I have to you and this house and my family. I give it all, so I have nothing left, Parker."

"I understand. That's why I said it's not you. Nothing you did. You're perfect. I love coming home to the house. I love coming home to you."

"So I'm supposed to live in this half-ass relationship? In this half-ass marriage? I don't deserve that. I deserve 100%. I give 100%, Parker. I give it every single fucking day."

"I know."

"I want to be with someone who does the same for me. I deserve it, Parker."

"You absolutely do."

If you're wondering how I have the exact dialogue from this conversation, I voice-recorded it on my old phone. How I knew to do that at that moment, I really have no idea. Listening back to it to put the dialogue in the book was hard. I ugly cried the entire time I listened to it. As strong as I was trying to be, I can hear myself lose that strength as the conversation continued. I so badly wanted this man to beg for me and to love me. He was a lost soul, and I was a pawn in his game.

Parker must have texted his best friend, Isaac, to come over because, to my surprise, Isaac walked through the door and into the war zone. He looked scared. I didn't want Isaac there, and I wanted Parker to leave too, so I asked him to pack a bag and leave. While Parker went upstairs to pack, Isaac asked me to go outside. I remember falling to my knees in the front of the house with my head in my hands as my body shook from crying so hard. Isaac tried to console me. He told me he had no idea, and he couldn't believe Parker would do this, but at this point, I didn't believe Isaac, and I honestly didn't care what he had to say.

Parker and Isaac got in the car and drove off. I went and sat in my sister's car outside of my house, and we talked for hours. We talked about every option I had and what the possible outcomes would be. My sister is my ride or die. She would've taken this to the grave if I didn't want anyone to find out. She would've stayed up all night with me. She said that no matter what I decided to do, she would support me. After all of the hours of crying, my body needed sleep. Vick offered to have me stay at her house, but I wanted to sleep in my own bed. She hugged me so tight before I got out of the car. The one thing I knew for certain was that my sister was going to be by my side no matter what was to come, and that brought me so much peace.

I can only imagine how hard it was for my sister to say that she would support me no matter what I chose to do and mean it after what she had watched me go through. We had a conversation not too long ago, and my sister said, "Sometimes I feel guilty that I didn't try harder to get you out of that relationship." But the truth is, I was going to do what I wanted to do. If she had tried to push me out of the relationship, I might have isolated myself from her. I had been at war with Parker every day since we'd moved into the house, and I needed my sister to be on my side, no matter what side that was (staying or leaving).

The next few weeks were a blur. Parker texted and called multiple times a day to apologize and tell me how much he loved me. He had been staying at his parents' house. He said he told them about what happened. I guess this is where I started to feel numb. I would reply to his messages with quotes that I found on Pinterest.

"Your marriage vows are most important in those moments when they are most difficult to keep."

"Without communication, there is no relationship. Without respect, there is no love. Without trust, there's no reason to continue."

"Breaking someone's trust is like crumpling up a perfect piece of paper. You can smooth it over but it's never going to be the same again."

"I don't know what I'm more afraid of: to see you again or to never see you again."

"Real men stay faithful. They don't have time to look for another woman because they're too busy looking for new ways to love their own."

One of the worst parts about all of this was that Allison and her husband, her father, and her mother were booked to attend our wedding. She would be sitting at our intimate, island wedding with her husband, watching her boyfriend take vows to me. Had she ever thought about how god-awful of a sin this would be? Would they have had sex in Aruba if I hadn't found out about their relationship weeks before? It made me fucking sick to my stomach to think about it. What kind of psychotic lunatics could do this?

I knew I needed to come to a decision quickly because the wedding was weeks away. I took a lot of time to think about what I wanted for myself. I wanted to be married for over thirty-five years like my parents. I wanted to have children and be a mom. I was so ready to enter this next chapter of my life. I just didn't know if that was with or without Parker.

I had two choices and neither felt good. If I called off the wedding and told my friends and family what was going on, there was no coming back from that. I knew I couldn't stay with Parker and have all of these people around me judging him and our relationship. It would be too big of a burden for me to carry. The other choice was to fight for this relationship. I could give him another chance. I could keep this huge secret from my family and friends and move forward.

My heart was torn because, despite his infidelity, he was my best friend, and my entire life was built around him. I'd known Parker since I was a little girl. I wish I could say that when you find something like this out, you automatically stop loving the person, but that just isn't the case. Every day spent away from Parker, I missed him. I couldn't imagine my life or future without him. I thought about the names we'd picked out for our future kids and our Sundays going grocery shopping together. I would regret not trying to make this work. I hated him for what he'd done, but my love for him was greater than my desire to leave the relationship, end the engagement, and call off the wedding. I had to follow my heart.

When I returned from Atlanta, Parker was living back in the house, and he had no idea what I wanted to do or what was coming next. When I got home, he met me outside to bring my luggage in. *Like he always did.* He looked terrible. He had dark circles around his eyes. It hurt me to see him like that. I walked into the house and went upstairs to shower, where I cried my eyes out. I'd had to keep this front on for the last five days while working, and I was so happy to finally be home. I could cry in my own shower and cry myself to sleep in my own bed. I got out of the shower and changed into comfortable clothes. I hadn't realized how much weight I had lost over the last week, but my pajamas were suddenly baggy on me.

Parker asked if I was ready to talk, and we made our way downstairs to the couch. We sat on opposite sides of the couch, and I immediately started crying and he did too. He looked so sad and lost, and that's exactly how I was feeling too.

He said, "Marissa, I am so sorry. I will do anything to prove to you until the day I die that it was a mistake, and it will never happen again. I swear on everyone that I love. I made a mistake. I wasn't thinking."

"How do I trust you?" I asked. "You don't even know why you did it in the first place. How can you know you'll never do it again? You can't. I've lost all my trust in you and my respect for you. How do we move forward?"

"I don't know. Maybe we put one foot in front of the other and try to repair this. I will do anything it takes."

"I want to believe you. I hope that you're telling the truth. I hope that this is repairable, but we won't know unless we try."

"I want to marry you, Marissa. There is no one else in this world for me. I made a mistake, and it will never happen again. Please believe me. Please let's move forward with the wedding. Let me prove to you that I can be a great husband."

As I sat there and stared at him, all I could think about was how much I loved him. Deeply, deeply fucking loved him. As I wiped the tears from my eyes, he said, "Can we still get married?" and I looked at him and said, "I don't want to call off the wedding. I don't want to let everyone down. I just don't know if this is going to work, but I'm willing to try."

I was exhausted and drained and needed to sleep. He said, "I don't have to sleep in the bed, but can I come sit with you for a little bit." I smiled and said, "I'm going to bed, Parker." I turned off the light on my nightstand and crawled into bed. The room was dark and peaceful.

It felt like I had no life left in me to fight. I had no clue what my future held and that scared the shit out of me. But it didn't scare me enough to make me leave. My desire to be chosen and loved by Parker always won. Unfortunately, I was in a lose-lose battle.

Chapter 6

I Am Getting Married

I WENT THROUGH with the wedding for two reasons. First, I had some glimmer of hope that we could pull through and make our marriage work. Somewhere in my hopeless-romantic mind and heart, I wanted to believe this was a one-time mistake and we could move through it. Second, I was too scared of what other people would think and what my life would look like if I broke it off. I couldn't face the external factors and the unknown. I didn't want to let my parents down. I didn't want to let my friends and family down because they had paid so much money to attend the wedding. I didn't want people to know I had been cheated on. I didn't want people to know there were cracks in the foundation of our relationship. I didn't want the picture-perfect vision of my life that the outside world saw to crumble to the ground. I didn't want to fail.

My desire to succeed in this marriage and not be seen as a failure outweighed everything else. It outweighed how horrible I felt, how alone I felt, how sick I felt. I knew if I moved forward with the wedding, I would face a lot less externally. It was like putting a Band-Aid on a bullet wound. But at the time, I didn't know I'd be slowly burying myself—my confidence, my self-worth, and everything that made me Marissa. But we live and we learn, right?

I knew it was a once-in-a-lifetime opportunity to have eighty of our closest family members and friends on our favorite island. I didn't want to let this dream go. The longer I stayed in my dream world, the less I had to face my own reality.

My dad was so excited for the wedding and to be on the island with our favorite people. He had a big cooler on the beach filled with beer and water, and everyone would go to his palapa for drinks. My parents had been with us every step of the way while we planned the wedding, and they were right there to watch this dream of mine come to life. They had no idea what Parker had done and were thrilled to gain another son.

The night before the big day, we got two coach buses from the hotel and headed up to Faro Blanco, a restaurant situated next to a lighthouse. As we entered the restaurant, the band was playing. The sun had just begun setting, and everyone was blown away by the view. Parker and I made our way to every table to chat with the guests. I remember looking over at my parents, and they were laughing. They seemed so incredibly happy, and nothing made me happier. We ate delicious food and cheered for our future.

On the bus home, I played "Don't Stop Believing" by Journey and the entire bus sang, "A singer in a smoky room. The smell of wine and cheap perfume. For a smile they can share the night. It goes on and on and on and on...." In that moment, I was so happy. I felt alive. I was surrounded by the people I loved the most. I don't remember if Parker was on my bus or the other one.

My sister slept with me that night. After she fell asleep, I lay there and thought to myself that I had an angel lying next to me. Her love was unmatched. Her love was unconditional. Her love had gotten me this far. I didn't know what the future held, but I knew my sister would go to the end of the earth with me if I needed her to, and I would never be alone.

The big day.

"A Thousand Years" by Christina Perri played as my dad walked me down the aisle. I remember holding his hand tightly and reciting the lyrics in my mind: "Darling, don't be afraid, I have loved you for a thousand years. I'll love you for a thousand more," and I knew I could pull through this. I knew the love of my parents and family would get me through this. I didn't know if I'd come out on the other side with Parker, but I knew I was strong enough to survive it. As we approached the altar, my dad kissed me on the cheek and gave Parker my hand in marriage. I don't remember most parts of standing at the altar with Parker, but I do remember when it was time for me to put the ring on his finger. He gave me the wrong hand, and everyone laughed. I remember thinking how crazy it was that our maid of honor and best man knew about Parker's infidelity and they had to stand beside us.

I do remember the reception! Parker and I were introduced as the new Mr. and Mrs., and we ran onto the dance floor as newlyweds. We danced to "(Everything I Do) I Do It for You" by Bryan Adams. As you can imagine, it was quite tough choosing a wedding song, but this one seemed appropriate. If you're not familiar with the song, it's about sacrificing everything for love and how love is worth fighting for.

In some crazy place inside of myself, I wanted to believe we could make it through. That our love was worth fighting for. I was hopeful we could turn this around.

The most perfect part of the night was when my dad and I danced to "Because You Loved Me" by Celine Dion, singing lyrics that spoke true to his endless, unconditional love for me. It's a moment I will cherish forever. I wish I could relive it a million times over.

My dad didn't know it at the time, but the love he and my mom shared was one of the main reasons I wanted to fight for my marriage. I had seen my parents go through tough times, and they always figured it out. They always chose each other. They hadn't gone through infidelity, but they'd struggled in other ways. Maybe this was just a bump in the road for Parker and me.

I danced the night away, one song after the next. I never left the dance floor. To be honest, I don't remember Parker dancing in the crowd of people. When the DJ played "Last Dance" by Donna Summer, I knew the magic of this night was coming to an end. I'd had so much fun. As the song ended, fifteen of us ran and jumped in the pool. I went in, wedding dress and all. It was the only way to end the night.

Parker and I spent the following week after the wedding in Aruba. I remember being thankful that a lot of family members and friends were still there vacationing because it took my mind off my own reality. I offered to pay to have my cousin and his wife stay for a few more days because I didn't want them to leave. They brought me so much laughter and peace that week, and I truly didn't want it to end, but they couldn't stay any longer.

One night, Parker and I went to dinner with his family, and we had a great time. His cousin told us about his travels around the world. He had such great energy, and I loved being around him. After dinner, we all walked back towards the hotel, and as we said goodbye, Parker's brother hugged us and said, "Hey, listen, I hope it all works out." This was the first moment where I had to face my new reality. The people who knew about Parker cheating would be hyper tuned into our life to see whether it would work out or not. I couldn't face this new reality. It was easier for me to push it all away and try to get back to our pretend perfect world. I couldn't even think about the fact that I was hiding this huge secret from my family because it made me sick. I felt like a fraud.

This trip and wedding was the start of me compartmentalizing as a coping mechanism. If I stayed in the "dreamy" parts of my reality, I didn't have to face the truth. If I moved forward with the wedding, I wouldn't face the external scrutiny, and everyone would be happy. If I sang one of my favorite songs loud enough on the bus ride back to the hotel, I wouldn't notice if Parker was there or not. If I stayed in the memory of my dad walking me down the aisle as I tightly squeezed his hand, I could block out the vows. If I didn't leave the dance floor, I could pretend I was anywhere else besides my wedding. If I jumped in the pool, I couldn't preserve my wedding dress. If I could convince my cousins to stay, I wouldn't be alone.

How long could I play pretend for?

Chapter 7

I Am Not Sure Who I Am Anymore

SOMETHING CHANGED IN me after I found out Parker had cheated. A part of me died. I tried so hard to find myself and my happiness, but I couldn't. The texts, pictures, and conversations played on repeat in my mind. My body was constantly in flight-or-fight mode.

Here's what the two years after the wedding looked like.

I never slept well after Parker cheated. When I did fall asleep, I would wake up in a panic and want to go through his phone. I would have nightmares about him cheating where I would scream and cry, but no words were coming out of my mouth. It was like no one could hear me.

I held all my stress in my shoulders, neck, and jaw and gained weight faster than ever before. Parker started to ask me every day if I was going to work out. He bet me new cabinets in our kitchen if I worked out with him for a month. I took the bet, I worked out with him every day, but the weight didn't come off. *And now he's not attracted to me, great!* I'm sure my cortisol levels were very high, and I wasn't sleeping, so it was nearly impossible for me to lose weight.

One weekend, I was in the kitchen washing dishes and Parker was in the garage. I heard this voice inside of my head tell me to go outside to the garage but to do it quietly. Again, this wasn't a scary voice. It was like a gentle, warm push towards something I needed to do. Low and behold, Parker was standing there with a vape in his mouth. And again, the milky yellow, see-through skin. Parker shoved it into a drawer. I was fucking furious. Why was he still hiding shit from me? I said, "You have to be kidding me," grabbed the vape from the drawer, and went into the house. I felt like a mother reprimanding her teenage son, except Parker was a grown fucking man. After a few minutes, he came inside and said that he needed to vape because it helped with his anxiety. It calmed him down. I started crying.

"Why are you still lying to me?" I asked.

"I don't know. I don't want you to be mad. Do you know what it's like to live up to your standards and expectations?"

In my head, I wondered if Parker was missing a moral compass of what's right and wrong. Was I too overbearing? Were my expectations too high? Did other husbands lie like this to their wives? Looking back now, we can put this into the gaslighting pile. Parker was saying it was my fault that he'd lied. And of course, it made me question myself yet again.

A few weeks later, I was cleaning the guest bedroom in our house, and Parker was showering. I heard that voice in my head tell me to search Allison's number in Parker's phone. He had left his phone charging on the nightstand, and I typed in her number, which I had saved in the notes section of my phone, and a contact named "Hello" came up. I couldn't see any messages, but we all know what this means. I sat on the bed and waited for him to get out of the shower.

"Why do you have Allison's number saved in your phone?" I asked when he came out.

"You're crazy, Marissa."

I showed him his phone, I showed him the contact, and he said, "I don't know why that's in there. Maybe from early on."

The only issue with that story is that I deleted and blocked her number from Parker's phone after our last interaction with her, so he would have had to unblock her and add it as a new contact. Parker changed the password on his phone after that fight, and I was never able to get into his phone again. That didn't stop me from looking. Sometimes I felt like a secret investigator, but he was getting good at hiding his tracks. I had seen some messages with girls on his World of Warcraft game. *How many girls were there? Did he have two cell-phones?* The questions I had went on and on.

In the fall, I received a promotion at my job, and I couldn't wait to share the news with Parker. When I got home from work, I ran up to his office to tell him, and his response made me feel like the promotion really wasn't that impressive or that big of a deal. It felt like everyone else around me was proud and was rooting for me, but Parker barely wanted to speak about it. He wasn't happy for my success at work and that hurt me. In the beginning of our relationship, we would talk about how much time and hard work we wanted to put into our careers so we could build a beautiful life and be successful. Now that my success had surpassed his, it felt like we weren't even batting for the same team. He wasn't even at the stadium where I was.

During one of our fights, we were sitting on the living room couch, and I said, "I feel like you don't love me anymore. You don't try like you used to. You don't ever say I'm pretty. You don't try to spend time with me." He blankly stared at me. I started to cry, and I said, "Maybe if I was less successful, you would love me more." He made a smart remark about how "successful" I was. I fucking hated the way he made me feel. I do not boast, and I would never make someone feel inferior. I truly felt that if I was less successful it would be one less thing that Parker would dislike about me. I later said, "Maybe if we have a kid, it will fix us."

Parker laughed and said, "I am not having a kid with you when we are barely able to go a few days without fighting."

He was right. When I think back to this fight and the words that came out of my mouth, I feel so bad for myself. I was pulling at straws to get this man's energy, affection, and time, and nothing worked.

In one of the many attempts to save my marriage, I said to Parker that we should book a weekend at the Mohegan Sun casino. We love to gamble, we hadn't been away in a while, and I thought we could both use a trip. He reluctantly agreed. We packed our week-ender bags into the car and headed to Mohegan Sun. While we were driving there, I thought about how much I loved our road trips. We hadn't taken one in years since Parker stopped going to car shows, and I missed the way we laughed in the car together. We would buy Red Bulls for the ride, and Parker would always finish his first, and then he'd start drinking mine, and I'd try to pull it away from him.

I felt so hopeful on the drive up. We checked into our room; it had a view of a beautiful lake. We had a nice dinner, we gambled, and I knew for sure that we were going to have sex that night. Well, I was wrong. I tried and he said he was too tired from the drive, and we could in the morning. When morning rolled around, he wasn't in the mood. *Great.* So we got up and did a little shopping. They had the cutest shops. This one Christmas store had these beautiful light-up snow globes and holiday scenes. We got two for our house and one for Parker's mom and grandma. They were going to love them! We gambled some more and had a nice dinner, followed by another sexless night. As we drove home, I knew him not wanting to have sex was a bad sign. I couldn't wait to get home and cry my eyes out in the shower.

The following spring, I was driving home from work, and I called Parker.

"Something has been bothering me lately," I told him. "I feel like you don't text me anymore during the day or even ask how my day is going. It's always me texting you and checking in."

Parker said, "We've been together for eight years. I don't need to fucking text you every second of the day. I have an important position at my company, and I can't text all day. Maybe you forgot about my position at work because you're only worried about yourself."

"I'm not asking you to text all day. I can't text all day either, but I would think you'd want to check in with me."

Parker yelled, "You're a boss, you shouldn't even be on your phone at work."

Click. The phone call ended. I wasn't far from home, but a part of me wished I wasn't going home. What if I got into a car accident that night and that was our last conversation? I bet if I was Allison, he'd be sexting me all day long. Wouldn't matter what his position was at the company. He was so fucking mean. You don't treat someone you love like that. When you care about someone, you check on them. I don't care how long two people have been together.

Later that week, I was lying in bed catching up on an episode of *Housewives* that I'd missed, and it was one of the very few nights Parker came into the bedroom before I was asleep. He got into bed and grabbed the remote. I said, "I'm watching this on demand, don't change it." He jumped out of bed, looked me dead in the eyes, and said, "Fuck you!" I didn't even know how to react. I was over his outlandish, childish behavior. I said, "That energy isn't welcome in my bedroom, so you can go downstairs and watch your show." He stormed out of the room and slammed the door.

When Parker and I first met, I was confident and held my own. I loved the way I looked and felt in my skin. I felt like I could take on the world. The first few years of our relationship, Parker made me feel like a queen. He put me on a pedestal. He made me feel like I deserved the best, finest things this life had to offer, and I believed him. At this point in our marriage, I felt so far from those feelings and that version of myself. I felt insecure, unworthy, timid, ugly, and fat. My relationship with Parker had beaten me down. It had taken the life out of me. I couldn't remember the last time I had seen my friends. All I did was work, spend time with Parker, and go see my family on the weekends. I was a shell of a person just barely getting through the day, and I needed help.

Chapter 8

I Am in Therapy

GROWING UP IN an Italian family, therapy wasn't necessarily encouraged. You just powered through the difficult times in life. It made you stronger, and you moved forward. Tomorrow is a new day. Amen. While that had been my approach all along with Parker, I couldn't ignore the fact that it was absolutely not working anymore. The relationship was taking a toll on me. I was at a dead end. I needed help. I needed to speak to a professional.

I begged Parker to do marriage counseling together or individual counseling for himself. He always said he didn't believe in therapy. One day when he was actually being honest with himself and to me, he said, "I don't want to go to therapy because I don't want to know what I would find out." Those words shook me to my core. It was the day I realized that Parker didn't trust himself, he didn't know himself, he didn't know what he was capable of, and he didn't want his skeletons dug up. All those skeletons were locked as deep and far away as possible, and that was fucking scary. I couldn't relate. As fucked up as this relationship made me, I still knew who I was deep down inside. I wasn't hiding anything. I genuinely needed help. I had exhausted everything within my power to try and help us, and I was getting nowhere fast.

The stars aligned on March 12, 2021, when I reached out to a therapist, Rachel Pedone, and she had availability to see me. Our first Zoom call was in the early evening during the week, and I took the call in my bedroom with the door shut. Parker was in his office next to our bedroom playing video games while I was on the call. Rachel's energy and voice felt so peaceful and welcoming. One of the first things that came out of my mouth was "I'm sorry. I don't even know where to start, but I need to save my marriage. What can I do?"

I walked Rachel through the previous three years and the current state of our marriage, and she knew way before I did that the end was near. Rachel knew Parker had checked out of the marriage many moons ago, and I was fighting a war that I wouldn't win. So, unbeknownst to me, Rachel changed the narrative, and we began working on me, the only person that we had control of. In session after session, we peeled back every layer of Marissa.

During one therapy session I will never forget, my therapist asked me to describe myself. I sat there puzzled and the only word I could think to describe myself was *generous*. I couldn't think of any other word. My homework that week was to look up some other adjectives to describe myself. In the notes section of my phone, I wrote *ambitious, thoughtful, honest, reliable, confident, trustworthy*, and *kind*. When it came time to read them out loud the next week in therapy, I could barely say them. I felt so far from the old Marissa that I once was.

For the longest time, I used to hate looking at myself in the mirror, and I would avoid them. Why? Because I didn't know the person looking back at me. I hated who I'd let myself become. If I kept avoiding the mirrors, I wouldn't have to sit with myself and my thoughts, and I did that for a long time, but therapy pushed me to overcome this. Every day, I would spend at least five minutes standing in front of the mirror and saying something nice to myself—congratulating myself on something I'd accomplished that day, crying and saying what I was feeling in that moment, staring at myself in silence, or complimenting my body. At first, I was so uncomfortable doing this. It was hard and the five minutes seemed to last forever. But as the days and weeks went on, I started to recognize myself again in the mirror. Staring at myself and talking to myself allowed me to become friends with myself again. I wasn't at war with myself anymore. I started to be comfortable with the person staring back at me.

As I navigated through what seemed to be a hopeless marriage, I was petrified of what came next. Through therapy, I learned to focus on what was in my control. There were a million things outside of my control, but I needed to find a peaceful place within myself and my reality that didn't feel like it was going to be ripped away. I made a list of everything that was in my control, and it helped to remove some of the heaviness and anxiety I was feeling.

The things that I felt were in my control were my thoughts, my daily routines, my job and financial stability, asking for emotional support from my family and friends, going to therapy, and putting one foot in front of the other.

We also talked about Parker of course, what was going on between us that week, and Rachel would give me the tools I needed to work through it. After each call, I would go into Parker's office and tell him all about it. I would say, we should try this or I need this from you and the marriage. He seemed like he was listening, but there was never any real action behind it.

One Wednesday night, Parker and I got into a blowout fight because he was trying to bring up things from past fights that still bothered him. After I'd found out Parker cheated, I said, "You're so lucky my dad and my brother don't know about this," and here we were two years later, and he was telling me that was a threat. He was scared of my dad and my brother, but they still had no clue about any of this two years later. They still thought the sun shined out of Parker's ass. Parker was trying to fight about anything and everything. At one point after he cheated, I said, "I don't know who raised you to be this way where cheating and lying is okay. Maybe your dad cheated on your mom and that's where you learned this." Two years later, he was still upset that I said that. Mind you, he never dealt with the fact that he'd cheated, but hearing me say that about his mom and dad sent him over the edge. What a fucking wild concept to comprehend.

I'd said those things because I was hurt. How could someone I love so much have been so careless with my heart, the life we'd built, and the eight years we'd spent together? Everything that Parker promised to change and do after he cheated seemed to be gone with the wind. Unfortunately, Parker showed me many times that he didn't care, and it was taking a mental, physical, and emotional toll on me.

When I was on the call with Rachel that week and shared the recent events, I could feel her tone towards Parker change. His behavior was unacceptable, and I needed to stand up for myself. I needed to start choosing myself. I needed to start seeing the bigger picture. Up until that point, I'd had tunnel vision, but now I was disgusted with his behavior too, and I was at the end of my rope. I had put in so much time and energy to communicate with him, actively taking everything I learned in therapy and applying it, and all it did was make him angrier. Maybe Parker hated me for getting help because he couldn't run anymore. I was no longer able to be convinced that I was crazy because I had a sound, third-party professional telling me otherwise, and I was finally starting to believe in myself again.

Chapter 9

I Am Calling It Quits

ON FRIDAY, MARCH 26th, I was working from home. I was pre-occupied with meetings, but I couldn't shake this unsettled feeling inside of me. My intuition knew something bad was about to happen. At 3 p.m., Parker texted me that he was going to his parents' house after work, and I knew deep down that meant he wasn't coming home. I replied, "Are you planning to come home later to have a conversation?" and he said he didn't know. I felt like I was in an alternate universe. *Was this the end? Was it really the end?* For a fleeting moment, I felt relief and everything around me felt quiet and calm. As I came out of that moment, I knew I had a mountain ahead of me that I couldn't climb alone and then the fear set in. *What does my life look like without Parker? Who is Marissa without Parker? My life has been built around this man. My life as I've known it is over.* The picture-perfect facade of a life and marriage was about to burn to pieces and it was time to let it burn. The tears started rolling down my face as I figured out what I had to do next. Naturally, I called my sister because she is my saving grace.

Vick answered, "What's up, Mariss?" I told her that Parker and I had been having a really tough time and that I thought it was over. "Like really over this time, and I'm ready to tell Mom and Dad," I told her. Vick asked if I was okay, if something else had happened. I said, "We've been fighting nonstop and it's the end. I know it's the end now." Vick asked if I was sure I wanted to tell Mom and Dad.

She knew all of the struggles and shit Parker and I had been through better than anyone else, but she also knew there was no coming back after I started to tell people. She was right, and I was finally ready for "no coming back."

I asked her if she could call Mom and tell her, and she said she would. Vick called my mom and merged me back into the call. She said, "Mom, it's me and Marissa on the line. There's something I need to tell you about Marissa. You should probably sit down." My mom, sounding nervous, asked what was wrong, and Vick said, "Parker cheated on Marissa, and they've been going through a tough time. They are splitting up." My mom asked if I was on the phone, and I said "yes", but I was barely able to speak through the tears. My mom said, "It's okay, Mariss. It's going to be okay. Come home."

I got into my car. I was barely able to see through the flood of tears, but I somehow made it to my parents' house. My dad was standing right there in the doorway as I pulled up. I ran inside and he hugged me, like really fucking hugged me, and I needed it so badly. He told me everything would be okay, that we would figure it out. And then my mom hugged me just as tight and said, "It's going to be okay, Mariss. You're home now." I sat down on their couch. For the first time in so long, I felt safe. Nothing or no one could hurt me anymore. The three of us sat together for hours and cried as I walked them through the hell and darkness that was the last two and a half years of marriage. I could see their hearts shatter for me when I told them about the affair before the wedding. Disbelief was written all over their faces. They were putting the pieces of the puzzle together in their minds.

My mom said, "Why didn't you tell us, Mariss? You didn't have to go through this alone."

"I didn't know what to do," I explained. "I knew if I told you guys, that Dad wouldn't be able to walk me down the aisle to this man. I never wanted to put you guys in that position. I didn't want you to hurt the way I was hurting, and you would have." My dad didn't have to say anything for me to know that it was true. He wouldn't have been able to give Parker my hand in marriage knowing how badly he had hurt me. They'd trusted Parker with my heart. They'd loved him like he was their own child. They'd expected more from him, and so had I. During this conversation, we realized Parker was not one of us. Our to-the-end-of-the-earth kind of love wasn't for everyone. And we don't hurt people we love. Yes, everyone makes mistakes, but some mistakes are too big to move on from. And maybe as hard as I tried to, I could never move past the infidelity and lies.

My mom asked, "Why did you play house for so long? You could have come home at any point."

I replied, "I don't know. I put my heart and soul into this man and our marriage. I didn't want to fail. I thought I could love him through all of his darkness and demons. I thought our love was strong enough to carry us through the hard times and it wasn't. And now I'm here. And I'm scared. He's been my entire life for eight years and now everything is changing."

"Well, it's only up from here," Mom said. "We are at rock bottom right now, and the only way out is up."

My dad agreed, saying, "We're going to figure this out. You don't have to worry. We're going to take this one day at a time."

And I knew they were right.

The waves of emotions were a rollercoaster between calmness, sadness, fear, contentment, heartbreak, anger, embarrassment, loneliness, disgust, and hope. I texted Parker a few times that night and tried to call him and Isaac, but there was no response from either of them. I reached out to my therapist, and we jumped on a call shortly after. I sat on my parents' bed and explained to my therapist about our fight during the week and how this had all unfolded. I felt so lost. My heart was hurting so bad. As we neared the end of the call, my therapist said, "Marissa, you know everything is going to be okay, right? You are going to be okay." And while it didn't feel like it at the moment, I trusted her. Those words gave me a glimmer of peace and hope while everything burned around me.

I stayed up all night and looked through every Instagram picture Parker and I had posted over the last eight years. I couldn't sleep and when I did drift off, I would wake up and realize the nightmare of my reality. My whole world had blown up. I was losing my best friend. I was losing someone who had been in my space and energy every single day for the last eight years. I was realizing how much I had lost myself. My mom was right...this most certainly was rock bottom. And I fucking hated it here. When the sun came up, I was still lying on my parents' couch. I hadn't slept for more than thirty minutes. I couldn't wait for my parents to wake up so they could sit there with me while I cried. I still hadn't heard from Parker. I felt like I didn't know which way was up or down.

My therapist now refers to these two weeks as crisis mode because we met nearly every day, and I was in bad shape mentally. We had a session that morning, and I cried so hard. I was so scared of how quickly my life was changing. It felt like I had just wasted eight years that I could never get back and I had to start all over again. My therapist reminded me that this life was mine. I had built this life. I still had a kick-ass job and a heart of gold. Yes, Parker had been a part of my life for eight years, but just because things had ended didn't mean my life went with it. Yes, things were going to change and change is never easy, but we were going to keep as much of my life the same as we possibly could. We were going to keep all of the good parts of my life and discard all of the bad parts. Let's call it spring cleaning. This conversation allowed me to start separating my life, my happiness, and my reality from Parker. I started to think about my life as a pie chart. Parker was one of those slices of the pie and, yes, that slice was being removed, but I still had this big, beautiful pie that was all mine. Before my therapy call that day, I was thinking of my pie as mine and Parker's, as if we shared a pie. But in fact we didn't. He had his pie and I had mine, and I was wildly grateful for that.

Later that day, my best friend, Katy, drove out to be with me. She took turns with my parents, consoling me. As the four of us sat in my parents' living room, I said to them, "I want to keep the house. The house is mine. Everything in it is mine. I decorated it. I made it a home. Parker lived in his office. He was a warm body in that house, but it's my home." My dad said that was no problem, if I wanted to keep the house, we would keep it. I felt a little less heavy after we came to that decision.

Then my dad said, "Divorces can be messy, and people act out of character during them. You are probably going to see sides of Parker that you wish you hadn't, but we will get through this. When you feel ready, let's go to the house and gather your items that are of value and bring them back here."

I'd already seen so many sides of Parker, what was a few more? I still hadn't heard from Parker. Mind you, he was probably at his parents' house just down the block from my parents' house, but he was choosing to ignore me. Seemed on brand for him.

Later that night, I felt strong enough to go back to the house and grab some things. My parents offered to come, but I felt okay with just Katy and I going. I knew Parker would see me enter the house on the camera and maybe then he'd choose to answer me and have a conversation. Moments after we walked into the house, Parker called. Our conversation was transactional and cold. I felt like I didn't even know who I was talking to, like he was a stranger. On this call, he said we could put the house on the market and split the difference. I told him I was going to keep the house, and I could feel his anger radiate through the phone. He was thinking that, in this housing market, we could sell the house for an outrageous price and split a few hundred thousand dollars between the two of us, but it wasn't about the money for me. It was about my peace. This was my home. I wasn't going to put it on the market. He asked why I would even want to stay there after we'd lived there and told me I couldn't afford that house on my own, but I didn't back down. He said, "I don't think that's a smart idea, but do whatever you want." I told him that after being together for eight years, I thought we owed it to one another to have a final conversation face-to-face, but he said he wasn't ready to have that conversation. Seemed all too familiar that the conversation would happen on Parker's time.

Katy and I gathered my belongings of value, and I packed them into my weekender bag. Parker always paid the bills in the house, and when I was going through documents in his office, I noticed there were bills due in a few days or overdue by a couple of days, so I knew another conversation was in the near future. Katy dropped me off at my parents' house and a part of me didn't want her to leave. She'd helped to put my mind at ease all day, and I was scared of what the rest of the night would hold. I lay down on my temporary bed on my parents' living room couch and cried. My life had changed so much in forty-eight hours, and I had no control over anything. My heart was aching. I missed Parker, the old Parker. I felt like I had this big, gaping hole in my heart. I wondered if he was sad or numb or scared too. Eight years of my life had vanished into thin air.

On Sunday, I called my boss. I work for a jewelry company based in New York City. I'd been with the company for eight years, and the owner of the company was a dear friend and mentor of mine. I called her and let her know what had happened and promised I would not let this affect my job. I just needed a few days to gather myself, and then I'd be back at work. She said, "Marissa, take the week off. Don't worry about work. Please take care of yourself and let me know if there is anything I can do to help." This was another conversation that gave me a glimmer of hope for the future. I loved my job and it wasn't going anywhere. Even on my worst days with Parker, I was always able to escape and go to work. It was my safe space and I loved being there. It was a place where I felt confident with what I contributed and brought to the table. While I might have lost most of my self-worth in my relationship with Parker, I was able to keep my self-worth at work. I never let my relationship issues affect my job. I was able to compartmentalize the two. I don't know how I did it, but I'm thankful I was able to.

I had therapy shortly after and was still trying to wrap my mind around how much had changed since Friday and how much more it was going to change. I'm not good with change, but when I was speaking to my therapist, I felt safe and hopeful, and I knew I could find the strength to push forward. Around 1:30 p.m., I got a notification on my phone that there was motion at the front door of the house. Parker had parked his car on a side street and climbed over the side railing on the front porch to attempt to enter the front door without being in the camera's view. It obviously hadn't worked. Then he pulled his car around to the front of the house and started to load his belongings into it. This experience made me feel so unsettled. *Why was he hiding? Why was he sneaking into the house? Why hadn't we had a face-to-face conversation? Was he scared to face me? How did we get here?*

During the following week, there was little to no communication between Parker and me. I woke up one morning and felt this overwhelming need to go to the house and take everything down that reminded me of Parker and the last eight years. My parents offered to come, but I knew I needed to do it on my own. As I stepped into the house, it felt calm and peaceful, an energy that I hadn't felt in the house in such a long time. The sun was shining through all the windows, and I started to feel okay. I shed some tears while taking down our wedding and vacation photos throughout the house, filling this big empty box with all our memories from the past eight years. Towards the end of the week, I knew I needed to get back into my normal routine, so I started sleeping at the house again and I went to work on Friday. It felt great to be back at work!

On April 8th, I called Parker to ask if we could meet in person. He didn't answer. I texted him the following day and asked what day and time worked to meet in person. I got no response. After work, I left the house to go have dinner with my parents. As I got onto Main

Street, Parker texted and said, "Where did you go?" because he'd seen me leave on the camera. I asked if he was coming to the house and he said yes, so I told him I'd turn around. As I waited for him to get there, my heart was pounding. I hadn't seen him and we'd barely talked since our split. Some crazy part of me thought there was a chance he'd say he made a huge mistake and wanted to fix this. That was obviously not the case. The fairy tale had long ago ended, my dear.

I was sitting on the couch, and Parker walked through the front door. He looked pale and had dark under-eye circles. He barely said hello and walked into the kitchen. He said he had to grab some more clothes and then we could talk. I said, "No, I'm leaving, so we can talk now, and you can grab your clothes after." He sat down on the couch directly across from me, and he was ready to talk business. In my mind, I'd imagined we'd apologize to one another, express that we both loved each other but ultimately it was time to move on. I thought we'd hug and cry and both get some sort of closure, but I was so wrong. Parker started talking about transferring all of the bills into my name, and the expectations he had about the house and lawyers, and how the next couple of months would go. I could have been talking to a stranger from the street at this point. This wasn't the man who had taken me through a five-hour proposal and asked for my hand in marriage. This wasn't Parker. In some fucked-up way, it made it easier to let go. The conversation was not more than fifteen minutes and then I left.

That week, we both took down all of the pictures of each other on our social media, and it was like our life together never existed. I watched his following count go up and up as he added all of these gorgeous girls on Instagram. I imagined he had been dying to do this for so long. He added one of my friends' friends, and my friend texted me and said, "Parker added Megan on Instagram. She just texted me a picture of the follower request and said, 'Isn't your friend married to him?' I told her you guys are breaking up and to run if he even tried to message her." I felt like I could puke. I knew continuing to follow Parker on social media would only hold me back from my healing, so I unfollowed him, his family, and his friends. It was time for me to move on.

I knew Parker and I were done for good, and I was coming to peace with that. The more time I spent away from Parker and in therapy, the more I could see him, myself, and our relationship in a different light. For the longest time, I'd blamed myself for his cheating, behavior, and choices, but I was finally starting to see clearly.

When someone needs external validation to feel happy, fulfilled, or secure, it's a slippery slope. In the beginning of our relationship, I was so in awe of Parker and in love with him, and it was the highest high for him. Then he moved onto expensive luxury cars. Everyone would congratulate him on his cars and, ultimately, his success at work that allowed him to afford those cars. Allison had her eyes set on Parker for a long time, and I can imagine how thrilling that was and how validated it made him feel. I wasn't giving him the attention he needed because I was wrapped up in picking out furniture for our new house and planning our destination wedding, and he found the attention he sought from Allison. It was the perfect storm. Allison wasn't happy in her new marriage and Parker wasn't the happiest at work, so they shared their unhappiness with one another, and it turned into a romantic relationship. Then I found out and it all went to shit. After that, I was no longer in awe of Parker. The validation he'd received from me in the past was gone. When we returned home from the wedding, Parker started to go to the gym or exercise at home for about two hours a night. He mentioned wanting to join a fitness competition. He purchased another luxury vehicle. The thing about external validation is that it always runs dry, and Parker knew it was time to run as far away as he could.

I began to realize how little self-worth I felt. My self-worth was always an extension of something else in my life, whether that be how much Parker loved me, how hard I worked at my job, how proud my parents were of me, or how good of an aunt, friend, or sister I was. I only felt good about myself when I was doing the most for everyone around me. And what happens when that's where your worth comes from? It isn't constant, and it's crushing when one of those sources disappears.

Spring and summer 2021 were difficult because Parker and I were navigating through separation. I was getting used to my new normal, but it felt like I had very little control. My aunt and uncle so graciously extended an invitation for dinner and "Dr. Phil Time" almost every day. Their house was on my way home from work, and it became a daily stop where so much of my healing took place. My uncle would walk through all different scenarios in my life and possible outcomes, so I was prepared for anything that could come my way. When I think back on this period in my life, that time spent with my aunt and uncle are my favorite. I always left their house feeling more like myself again and one step further in my healing journey. I'm forever thankful for the months we spent together.

One of the more positive things that came to light during our separation was that our marriage license from Aruba was not valid and held no legal significance here in the states. This was the best news I could have ever received because we would not have to go through a divorce or pay Parker a percentage of my assets or alimony. I would buy him out of the house and that would be the end of it!

Parker was taking his sweet time moving out of the house, and he made it known that he was allowed there whenever he wanted until we closed on the house and it was only in my name. He was right, that was the law, but it wasn't easy seeing him. It was like I was stuck in this dimension between my old life and my new life. He would come by the house unannounced, and I hated that. I always made sure to lock my bedroom door while I was sleeping or changing and the same for the bathroom because he would just pop up. He was at the house every weekend washing his cars in the driveway, waving hi to the neighbors, and pretending he still lived there. Our life together was over, but he made the most out of every waking moment he was still on the deed of the house. It drove me fucking crazy.

One Friday afternoon when I was working from home, Parker came by and went upstairs to continue packing. I had just received a new dress that I planned to wear to my niece's birthday party that weekend, and he came downstairs and said, "Is that a new dress? Do you have a date this weekend?" *How dare you ask me that? You've got some fucking nerve.* I replied, "Wouldn't you like to know!"

My niece's birthday party was the first event I'd attended without Parker. All my friends and family were there, and it felt like everyone was staring at me, like they all felt bad for me. Every hello had an added "You doing okay? Are you hanging in there? You know I'm here if you want to talk." I hated the pity. I used to walk into a party with a beautiful outfit on, my head held high, and not a care in the world. I was so far from that Marissa.

In the following weeks, I did my best to put one foot in front of the other and do things that made me happy. I reconnected with my friends. I began to go out for dinner and drinks again. I shopped for new clothes. I started to ride bikes with my aunt down by the water. I got back into paddle boarding. I spent a ton of time down by the beach, a place where I feel most at peace.

One of my favorite self-care methods was taking a warm Epsom-salt bath with lavender-scented bubbles. One Sunday afternoon, I locked the bathroom door and got into the bath. As I drifted into my state of relaxation, I heard a startling bang on the bathroom door. I jumped out of the bath and stood there naked and frozen in place. I heard Parker say, "Can you move your car? I need to wash mine in the driveway." I watched the door handle jiggle. *Was he trying to get into the bathroom? What the fuck was wrong with him?* I looked at my phone and realized I hadn't received a notification of movement at the front door. Conveniently, the camera was turned off. I said, "Go downstairs, I'll be down in a minute." When I got downstairs, I said, "You need to tell me when you're coming to the house. I am a single female living here, and you just scared the shit out of me. And it's inappropriate for you to be seeing if the bathroom door is open." He said okay, but it was clear he was going to do what he wanted to do.

One Saturday, I went to spend time with my siblings, my cousin and his wife, and their children. It was the second time I'd seen my cousin since Parker and I split, and we were able to make light of the situation. We had a lot of laughs that day. I remember my cousin saying, "I never told you this, but I was at a restaurant in Port Jeff a few months ago on a Wednesday during the workday, and Parker walked in to pick up a to-go order. I think he saw me, but he pretended like he didn't, and he walked out quickly." I was so confused because Parker worked forty-five minutes from Port Jeff. Why was he there during the middle of a workday? Then I remembered who lived in Port Jeff—Allison. I was at the point where these sorts of stories didn't make me want to puke anymore. They validated that Parker had been lying and doing sneaky shit right up until the end.

One Sunday, Parker came by to get my engagement ring. I wasn't sad giving it back to him because the Parker that had proposed with that ring wasn't the Parker standing in front of me. I finally felt okay with that. He asked if I wanted to buy the ring from him, and I just started laughing. What the fuck was I going to do with that ring?

I was traveling for work a couple weeks later, and I got a notification that there was motion at the front door. I opened the app, and I could see Parker installing another camera next to our original camera. I was furious. Why the fuck was he installing another camera? It was a matter of weeks before we closed on the house. I called my parents, and my dad said he'd go over there. I watched as my dad's car pulled up. At this point, Parker was in the backyard. My dad opened the gate, and I could hear them exchanging words. Parker said he didn't know who I had coming into the house, so he needed to install his own cameras. I believe Parker had three or four cameras, but he only installed two. I wondered if he had cameras in the house that I didn't know about. I wondered why he cared who was in the house. He didn't have anything of value in the house anymore, so what was the difference? None of it made sense.

We were two weeks out from closing on the house, and I could finally see the light at the end of the tunnel. One of the only times Parker announced that he was coming by the house was when he and Isaac were coming to do a final sweep for his things. Parker reached out to me on Friday and told me he and Isaac would be by the house around 9 a.m. the following day. It was Saturday morning, and my dad came by the house to supervise. I was sitting in my bed when I heard Isaac's truck pull up, and I looked out my bedroom window. I instantly felt so sad. Parker had been by the house so many times, and I'd never felt this way. It was the finality of it. As happy as I was to close this chapter out, it didn't wash away the fact that Parker had been in my life since we were kids. He had been my best friend and part of my family for so many years, and I was going to miss him.

I've learned that it's okay to miss someone even if they hurt you. It's okay to acknowledge the love you had for someone even if that love is no longer. It's okay to wish someone the best even if they couldn't give that to you. It's okay to pray for people who need it most. I've learned that some people are only meant to be in our lives for a certain period, and we have no control over how long that time is. We can't take everyone with us on our journey forward, and it's okay to be sad when we must leave people behind. It's okay to free yourself of people, places, and things that no longer align with you. It's okay to be free.

Chapter 10

I Am Free

YOU KNOW THAT feeling when you can finally unclench your jaw and let your shoulders roll down and back? It had been so long that I barely remembered this feeling, but it was back, and it felt so damn good.

In August, Parker and I sat across from each other at the lawyers' office as we closed on the house. I remember looking over at him and thinking he was a stranger. I'd known him for almost my entire life, and now I had no idea who this man was. The lawyers were handing us papers to sign and date. After we finished signing, my dad rubbed my back, and I knew that meant, "This is over." When we wrapped up the meeting, my dad and I stood up from our chairs and walked out of the lawyers' office with our heads held high. We didn't say goodbye to Parker. When we reached the car, my dad gave me the biggest, tightest hug.

"I'm so proud of you," he said.

His "I'm so proud of you" went way beyond me being a single, female homeowner at thirty. It was an acknowledgement of making it through the heartbreak and betrayal. I didn't only make it through, I came out on top with my dignity. And maybe that's what happens to good people. You make it through the things that were sent to destroy you. You grow stronger and you don't lose sight of who you are and what you stand for. I will always be "good people," and that is something I am so proud of.

We were meeting my mom, aunt, and uncle for a celebratory dinner afterwards. As I drove to the restaurant, I felt light. Lighter than I'd ever felt before. I felt like I had been carrying the weight of the world and Parker for so long, and I was so happy to finally set it down and set that shit on fire. It was no longer mine to carry, and I never wanted to carry it again. I was never going back to that place of darkness. I made a promise to myself on that drive to dinner that I'd never lose myself again, and I'd never stay where I no longer belonged. Deal? Deal.

The restaurant was right on the water, and we had a beautiful view of the sunset. My glass of wine was perfectly chilled. We toasted to getting a second lease on life and love. I felt so happy and hopeful for the future. I was so damn proud of myself. When I pulled into my driveway that night, I turned off the car, looked up at the sky, and said, "Thank you" with tears rolling down my face. I knew I had an entire squad up there that was in my corner, and they had gone to war for me. Victory at last. I opened the front door to my house. Yes, *my* house. How cool was that?! I went upstairs to my bedroom and didn't have to lock the door behind me for the first time in a long time. I got into bed and drifted off into the most peaceful, deepest sleep I'd had in years.

The second I put that chapter of my life to bed, the universe was ready to let the blessings pour in.

Fall of 2021 was such a special time for me. I was finally feeling like myself again. Everything around me was settling into place. I redecorated the house and made it feel like home again. In my bedroom, the guest room, my new office, and the backyard, I created spaces that I loved being in. My home became my sanctuary. I, of course, saged the entire house because only good energy was welcome from here on out.

I had lost over thirty-five pounds with little to no exercise or changes in my diet. Once the stress of the relationship and closing on the house was gone, the weight went with it. After I'd found out about the infidelity and lies, the weight gain happened so quickly. One minute I was at my normal weight and the next minute my world had come shattering down and I gained thirty pounds. I was so hard on myself about gaining weight. Not for one second did I think it was because of everything I was going through. I thought it was because I wasn't exercising enough or I needed to eat less, but I tried doing everything to lose weight and nothing changed. I know there are other people out there that will read this paragraph and relate, and I want you to know that you're not alone. I wish I had shown myself some grace back then, but I wasn't capable of that at the time and that's okay. My weight doesn't define me. Your weight doesn't define you. Let's make a pact together that we will show our bodies grace during every season of our lives, and we'll do our best to live in alignment by removing the people, places, and things that no longer deserve a place in our lives.

I had this overwhelming calling to start writing a book. I didn't know why or how to start, but I did. I figured at the very least, it would help me heal. The truth is, I've never been a big book reader. I read one book a year while on vacation. My mom and sister both read fifty books a year. Me writing a book was a little out of left field, but so was everything else that had gone on the past few years, so let's add it to the list. I spent my nights after work and the weekends writing the book. Having to walk through the best and worst memories from the previous ten years was not easy. As a more healed version of myself, I found myself feeling bad for the person I'd been when I was with Parker. That girl was helpless and trying so hard to make her marriage work, but she had completely lost sight of herself, her self-worth, and her own happiness. It broke my heart. There were nights I'd be in bed with my laptop writing, and I'd start crying so hard that I had to shut my computer and come back to it a few days later. Especially hard was writing about the night I found out Parker had cheated. I still hate that night.

Most times when I would write, I was in awe of how far I'd come and the life I'd built for myself. It was extraordinary. Having to revisit these memories and write them down was a game changer in my healing. I was able to walk through the darkness again and into the light and heal through it. I know I'd handle so many of these scenarios differently now than I did back then. I guess the saying is true: "Do the best you can until you know better. Then when you know better, do better." My only goal was to do better.

One day I went to get my haircut and my normal hairdresser was out, so they said they were going to have someone named Ashley cut my hair. When I saw Ashley walk in, I realized we had gone to high school together. It had been years since I'd seen her, but way back when she was a mutual friend of mine and Parker's. I was excited to see her. I sat down in her chair and congratulated her on her engagement. I had seen the beautiful pictures on social media and was so happy for her. She excitedly walked me through how her fiancé proposed and where they wanted to have their wedding. She was so incredibly happy. *I remember being that happy too.*

After she finished telling me all the details, she said, "If you don't mind, I must ask what happened with Parker. You don't have to share if you don't feel comfortable."

I smiled at her in the mirror and said, "Parker and I were together for a long time, and I thought he was my person, but I was wrong. About a month before our wedding, I found out he was cheating on me with his boss's daughter, who was also his coworker, and that was the beginning of the end."

Ashley looked like she'd seen a ghost. She said, "No, wow, no. I had no idea. I'm so sorry, Marissa."

"Me too, but it's for the best. I truly am the happiest I've ever been in my life. It wasn't meant to be and that's okay."

"I commend you," she replied. "I don't think I'd be able to speak so nicely about someone who did that to me. I'm sorry, I just can't believe that. Parker was always in love with you, ever since we were young. You were his dream girl. I remember thinking Parker finally got his girl when you two started dating."

As I listened, it brought me right back to the night Parker kissed me on my parents' steps. To the days when we held hands under blankets or hid together during manhunt so we could sneak more kisses behind a tree. To the year that he pursued me, but I wanted to be single. To finally becoming his girlfriend and feeling like the stars had aligned for us. The last few years had been so rough that I had forgotten about the magic in the beginning. *It was real, wasn't it?*

I looked at Ashley through the mirror and said, "I know. I never thought Parker would do what he did, but people change."

"I don't even know if I should share this but a couple of months ago, in July, I was at the winery with my fiancé and when I walked in, I saw Parker and a blonde-haired girl," Ashley told me. "We made eye contact, and he looked like he'd seen a ghost."

I said, "I know that look, unfortunately."

Ashley laughed and said, "I texted my best friend Ellie because she, Parker, and I used to hang out all the time and I said, 'You're never going to believe this, but Parker is at this winery and he's not with Marissa. He's with some blonde chick.' Ellie told me to take a photo of them so we could send it to you. I somehow managed to get a photo, and I was going to message you on Instagram, but then I saw you had taken down all your pictures of you two. I could tell you guys had broken up. I'm pretty sure the blonde girl is his girlfriend now."

I said, "His next victim" and we laughed.

In September, I went on a girl's trip to Scottsdale, Arizona, with two friends. It was my first girls' trip in over ten years and, all I know is, whether you're single or married or it's complicated, girls trips are a must. They are good for your soul. On that trip, I felt like I was connecting with this new version of myself. A version that was present in the moment, soaking up each second, laughing until she cried, drinking one too many margaritas, and finally living life for herself.

In October, my boss scheduled my performance review. The previous few months had been so crazy, I hadn't even realized it was that time of year. A few minutes into the meeting, she told me that I was getting promoted to Vice President of Wholesale. Tears flooded into my eyes. I was so grateful to her and the company for believing in me and for rewarding my hard work. It was such an honor to get this promotion. My job had saved me in more ways than one. It was my escape from reality when I was with Parker, and it was my safe, familiar, and steady place when Parker and I broke up and everything felt like it was changing. It truly felt like my dreams were coming true.

The day after I got the promotion, I left on vacation to Aruba with my parents and Katy. It was my first time back there without Parker, and it was time to reclaim my island and happy place. And that's exactly what we did! The crystal-clear water, cool breezes, ice-cold strawberry daiquiris, and tranquil state of mind were perfect for celebrating this new, beautiful lease on life. The good-looking men at the bar paying us a little too much attention didn't hurt either.

While we were on the beach one day, there was a video on my TikTok of a woman walking on a beach telling her story about how she had been cheated on. She talked about the heartbreak that comes when the person who vows to love you cheats. How the person you thought you knew and loved is more like a stranger. How the web of lies goes on and on. She thanked her ex-husband for being so careless that she was able to find out he was cheating, for not waiting until they had kids, and for showing his true character after five years instead of ten. She thanked him for setting her free. She forgave the woman he cheated with. She thanked her family for their support through the toughest time in her life. She could have been telling my story with Parker, and every word gave me chills. A video has never resonated more with me than this one. I asked my mom to watch it, and a few seconds in I could see her eyes filling up with tears. I grabbed her hand tight and said, "Don't cry, Mom, I'm so happy now," and she said, "I know, but I hate that we had to go through that." The truth was, I was so grateful. That chapter in my life had to end so I could enter the most beautiful chapter yet. The chapter where my dreams really do come true.

Up until that point, I hadn't shared anything about the breakup or cheating on social media. I just removed all the pictures of Parker and continued as if our life together never existed. I finally had the courage to share this video to Instagram. I finally wasn't embarrassed of Parker's cheating because it had nothing to do with me. This was my story, this was my truth, and I was ready to share it. The outpouring of love and support I received after posting the video was unbelievable. I didn't realize how many people I was friends with on social media had been through something similar, and we were able to connect about it.

Until then, I didn't know if I would publish this book or keep it to myself, but on that day, I knew I needed to publish it. It's not that big of a world after all. Everyone is fighting their own battles and doing their best. Connection is such a beautiful privilege, and I wanted everyone that reached out to me to know that they were not alone. I guess I had, unknowingly, turned into the person that I needed most when I found out Parker cheated on me. Back then, I was so scared of the future and what people would think. Now, being authentic to myself and my story and being vulnerable allowed me to connect with many people on such a deep level. I couldn't help but think, *Maybe this is what I was meant for.*

Chapter 11

I Am a Psychic Medium

SPEAKING OF WHAT I'm meant for! I bet you didn't see this one coming. I know some of you reading this right now are picking your jaws up off the floor. I had to as well when I realized what these gifts were. Was I born psychic? I'm not sure. I didn't see ghosts as a child or an adult. *Thank goodness.* I've always been able to pick up on people's emotions and energy, and sometimes they'd linger within me. I have always been an empath and an intuitive, and I've always wanted to help people. Connecting with people on a soul level makes me feel alive.

Shortly after Parker and I broke up, I met with a psychic. I had never been before because I was always too scared they'd tell me I was dying or I was with the wrong man, but now I had nothing to lose. I probably could've used the guidance eight years before, but then I wouldn't be writing this book. Anyway, the only information she knew was my name and email address. We got onto the Zoom call, and she said, "Your heart is heavy, your energy is drained, and you're scared of the future. The person you just got out of an eight-year relationship with was not a soulmate, but a karmic partner. He was put into your life to teach you lessons, but you allowed him to overstay his welcome. The universe tried to show you so many times that he was not meant for you, and you ignored them. You could see in his eyes that there wasn't a sound soul inside of him, and you thought you could love him through it. No one can."

She connected to my grandmother and my two grandfathers. She mentioned that my grandmother was my guardian angel and, although she had passed away when I was very young, my story and hers were very similar. She said my grandmother was so proud of the way I'd made it through, and she wished she'd had that same strength when she was here on earth. She said my mom's dad is the bird that knocks at my window. I couldn't believe she'd said that because when I am sitting in bed, especially on the weekends, there is a bird that constantly knocks at my bedroom window and sometimes I say, "Enough! Stop tapping at my window." I felt bad now that I was telling the bird to go away, knowing it was my grandfather. He also said he loves the picture that I have of him in the guest room, and he is with me when I look at that picture. There is no way in hell this woman could know I had a photo of my grandpa in the guest bedroom. My dad's father also expressed how proud he was. He said he is the white feather. I see white feathers all the time, especially when I'm with my dad.

Towards the end of the call, she blurted out, "You're psychic, you know that, right? You can hear spirit. Clairaudient, but you will have all the clairs." I said I didn't think that was me, and she said, "Get up and go look at his Apple Watch." I felt my stomach drop. *How did she know that? Who even said that to me? Did I say that to myself? What does clairaudient mean? I have clairs? What are clairs?*

She said, "He was depleting you of your energy and gifts, so it's going to take some time to get them tuned up again, but they'll be back. I promise."

I was so confused. She told me I was going to spend years healing and finding myself. I would eventually meet my soulmate and, right before I met him, a seagull would drop something right in front of me on the beach. Within days, Mr. Right would be introduced. She said that everything I touched would turn to gold. I imagined she ended every call saying that.

It sure as hell didn't feel that way though. I left that call feeling like my mind had been blown. *I'm not psychic...am I?* I couldn't stop thinking about our conversation. The following week I got a package in the mail from the psychic. It was a deck of tarot cards. I had to look up what a tarot card deck was. Tarot is said to have originated in Northern Italy. It's a beautiful divination tool used to help connect you with your highest self, your spirit team, or the higher astral realm. In doing so, you can read energy, get the answers you seek, and predict what's to come. I was quite confused, but I started shuffling. Once I caught on to shuffling, I learned how to pull the cards. I researched and studied each of the card's meanings. I would ask a question out loud, and my spirit team would respond by having certain cards flip out to answer my question.

I started to realize that my spirit team had been communicating with me and guiding me the entire time I was with Parker. Yes, I ignored a lot of it, but I did listen when they told me to go look at his watch or go into the garage. They were pushing me to go see the truth. Although I ignored their signs once I got there, I can't deny that they were with me every step of the way.

In November 2021, something devastating and traumatic happened. One of my best friends, Danielle, lost her fiancé, Vinny, in a car accident. I'll never forget that day. Danielle's sister Jenn texted me with the news. I immediately couldn't breathe. *How could this be?* Vinny was this bigger-than-life kind of person. He treated Danielle like a queen. They were getting married in four weeks. *How could this be?* As tears rolled down my face, I could hear someone say, "Get the deck." I grabbed the tarot deck and two cards fell out. The Death card and the ten of swords. Both symbolize an ending. I felt chills. On the bottom of the deck was the nine of cups, and I could hear the words "He lived life to the fullest. He lived and he loved. Danielle showed him true love. One of his last wishes here on earth." I couldn't believe this. I couldn't believe Vinny was gone, and I couldn't believe they were saying this to me.

I will spare you the gut-wrenching days, weeks, and months that followed Vinny's passing, but I knew without a doubt in my mind that my gifts had been ignited so I could help him communicate with Danielle. And that's what Vinny and I have done ever since. He's part of my spirit team and I know him better now than I ever did when he was here on earth. I've helped Vinny deliver messages and physical gifts through me to Danielle. For instance, one night Vinny came through when I was lying in bed, and he wanted Danielle to know that their dog Swisher would be okay. Danielle was leaving on a trip in the morning, and he told her to have a Bahama Mama for him. He had some other messages for me and by the time I finished communicating with him, it was too late to text Danielle. At 5 a.m., I texted her and said, "I hope you have a great trip and a safe flight. Vinny came through last night and wants you to know Swisher will be okay. Is everything okay with Swisher? He also wants you to have a Bahama Mama for him."

Danielle immediately texted back and said, "Swisher has been throwing up since 2 a.m., and I'm so nervous about leaving. I'm so glad he said Swisher will be okay. I was thinking about canceling the trip."

Sure enough, Swisher was okay, and Danielle ended up having an awesome trip. Another fun thing happened one morning when I was getting into my car to drive to work. Vinny came through and said, "Tell Danielle to keep an eye out for a rainbow sticker on the back of a car this morning. That's the sign I'm sending her." I texted Danielle and let her know. Within an hour, Danielle texted me back and said she had just seen a big rainbow heart sticker on the car in front of her and that she'd needed that that morning. It's in these small moments that my gifts have given Danielle some peace of mind, hope, and the knowledge that Vinny is never too far away. If I can be Vinny's vessel here on earth to bring these messages and guidance to Danielle, there is nothing in the world that I want more.

At the beginning of my spiritual journey, I thought the voices in my head were my own. I know you are saying maybe you should check yourself into a mental institution, but I promise, I am mentally sound. I would hear these voices in my head, different voices, they weren't all the same. For instance, Vinny sometimes talks with a heavy Italian accent if he's trying to be funny. I would also have songs playing in my head. Early on in one of my therapy sessions, before I uncovered my gifts, I asked my therapist if having an inner dialogue was common, and she assured me that it was.

When I was first uncovering my gifts, I said to my sister, "Do something or move something in your house tomorrow so I can see what spirit shows me." The next day, I texted her and said, "I'm seeing daisies." Mind you, my sister does not buy flowers. Her husband buys her flowers for special occasions, but this was a normal Saturday morning. She responded with a picture of colorful daisies in a vase on her counter that she had bought at the grocery store, and right then and there, she was a believer! I guess I was starting to be a believer too.

I do want to give a quick shout-out to my sister because I've really put her through the ringer these past few years. She was the first person I called when Parker cheated, she had to help me decide if I was having a wedding or not, she had to call my mom to tell her Parker and I were breaking up, she had to help me pick up the pieces of myself after the breakup, and then when I got on the other side of that chaos, I tell her I'm a psychic medium. She deserves a round of applause for her unconditional love and support in every season of this life. Everyone needs a Victoria in their life!

When I started to acknowledge my gifts, I opened up to my therapist about it. Was she caught off guard? Probably. But she made me feel safe in sharing this. I talked more about the inner dialogue and how much of it I had. I could see my therapist understanding on a deeper level that it was a lot more than just an inner dialogue. I asked her if it's common to have songs pop up in your mind and play and she said, "It's not, but that's most likely part of your gift." That same night, I felt her aunt come through and I shared this with her. Her aunt was showing me a doll with these two pigtails that stick out straight on each side of her head. My therapist shared that her aunt had left her a nutcracker that looked exactly like that before she passed away. We were both blown away.

My gifts are continuously developing, and I'm learning more and more about this part of myself. I can connect with my spirit team and ask for guidance at any time. I started out reading for friends and then they told their friends and family, and next thing I knew, I'd read their entire family. It's truly so special.

I have set boundaries with my spirit team because I work a corporate job during the week, so now they ring my ear when they want to come in and chat. When I'm home at night or during the weekend, they communicate as they please. We have a good, mutual understanding of our boundaries. Sometimes they slip up and start singing a song for someone in the room when I'm in a meeting, or a passed loved one wants to talk to someone I work with, but I say "not now" in my head, and they stop.

I'm able to connect with my loved ones that have passed as well as the loved ones of the person I'm reading for. It's almost like they sit in a waiting room, ready to talk. It's so cool! Being able to connect the reader to their loved ones that have passed is so special to me because their loved ones want to acknowledge specific memories as well as bring them guidance. It's like being on a telephone to heaven, and I just happen to be the cord between the reader and the person who passed away. So many people fear death, whether it be the death of their loved ones or their own passing, and there truly is nothing to fear. We are not making it out of this life alive, but your loved ones that have passed over are always around you and always guiding you. And when you need to hear from them, or when you need an answer or guidance, you can ask them yourself or you can seek the guidance of a psychic medium. Sometimes when I'm driving to work, if I have a quick question, I'll say, "If I should do this, please show me a big thirty-one," and within one minute there is a huge thirty-one on the back of a massive semi-truck, and I know it's a yes! Or it's another number and I know it's not the right move to make. They will show you the answers you need to know even if you don't have psychic abilities. You just need to ask and trust in the higher realm.

I know you're probably thinking I must have all the answers for myself then too, right? The answer is not really. Spirit doesn't show me very much for myself. When I ask for guidance, they are there to help me, but they want me to move through life like everyone else. Do I have a sneak peek at what's to come? Sometimes. But overall, my gifts are to be shared with my clients and that fulfills me so much. Do I wish they'd show me when Prince Charming was coming in to sweep me off my feet? Yes, I certainly do, but they are saving that for now, and I'm okay with it. I trust them.

I truly believe in divine intervention and divine timing. Divine intervention is when the universe, or whoever you believe in, steps in and moves some pieces around in your life so something magical and miraculous can occur. It's a moment in time when you say, "Wow, this cannot be a coincidence." Because it's truly not. I believe that divine intervention has taken place many times in my life.

One of the most obvious examples of divine intervention for me was Parker not coming home on the day we decided to end the marriage. The fact that it was a clean break with little to no communication was exactly how it needed to unfold so I could close that door once and for all. Another is that our marriage license in Aruba was not valid. Another is my promotion at work to VP of wholesale right after I closed on my house and would be paying every bill on my own.

Another beautiful example of divine intervention was when I felt called to get a psychic reading from this woman I had seen on Tik Tok, Gemma Lonsdale. I had watched many of her videos and loved her energy, and I wanted to have her read for me. We got on a Zoom call at 7 a.m. on a Monday morning, and Gemma's energy radiated through the screen. As soon as she started reading me, she took a minute to listen to what her spirit guide was bringing to her. She said, "I've never had this come in before, but my spirit guide wants us to work together. They want me to coach you." I was caught off guard but intrigued. I had looked at her mentorship program while browsing her website before booking a reading. I asked how much it would cost to have her coach me, and she said it would be free of charge. She told me that one day I would mention her name, and it would bring her so much abundance. I didn't know what that meant, but I felt so grateful to her.

From that Monday on, we met every two weeks via Zoom, and Gemma helped me to strengthen my gifts, build a website, and create a true business out of my readings. She has also offered unlimited guidance along the way. In one of our more recent sessions, Gemma mentioned that her birthday was in January. I told her mine was as well and asked her what day. She said "January 31st" and my jaw dropped to the floor. I said, "So is mine!" Neither of us could believe it, but then again, we could because we believe in the universe and that we were always meant to be on each other's paths. I am so thankful for Gemma and her guidance. I will be mentioning her beautiful name in every room I enter for many years to come.

My gifts have allowed me to connect with people from all around the world. I've had the honor of telling people they are pregnant before they even know themselves or that they would be getting pregnant before they conceived. I've helped men and women get out of relationships or jobs that they were no longer meant to be in. I've shared the exciting news of upcoming job promotions, career changes, new love, new opportunities, and vacations. I've also shared some uncomfortable information of there being a third-party energy in a relationship or marriage. I've worked with hundreds of people that are in the dating scene to check on the energy of their current connection, what's to come, and if it's worth pursuing further. Bringing guidance and clarity to the people I read for is a gift. My gifts are so sacred and special to me, and not a day goes by that I am not sending a huge shout-out and thank-you to the universe and my spirit team for allowing me to have these beautiful gifts.

Sometimes I can't help but wonder, why me? Why was I chosen to have these gifts? Why did I write this book? And in those moments, I think back to when I was a young girl or who I was when I was with Parker. I really could've used some spiritual guidance. I could've used a book that made me feel less alone, that made me believe I could make it through difficult times, that helped me to heal, and that allowed me to see there is happiness after rock bottom. I, unknowingly, have turned into the person I needed most my entire life. Maybe this is my path because I'm here to show others that mountains can be moved. Maybe my life purpose is to help guide others through their healing and spiritual journeys. Maybe I'm meant to touch the world and the people in it, in a special way. Maybe I'll leave this world a better place than before. That's all I could ever hope for.

Part 2

My Healing Journey

I THINK OF my healing journey as a long, winding road. When I made the promise to myself that I was going to prioritize my healing and find myself and my happiness again, that was the moment when I started my journey down the road. One foot in front of the other. Some days it rained, other days it was sunny. Some days my feet hurt and I wanted to stop walking. Other days I ran. Some days I cried, other days I smiled from ear to ear. Despite the conditions, I never gave up. I never gave up on myself.

Here's the map of my road to healing so far:

1. Getting to know myself
2. Forgiving myself
3. Accepting myself
4. Protecting myself
5. Aligning myself
6. Being the best version of myself

Along the way, I've learned that healing isn't linear. The road that is this healing journey stretches on forever. There is no final destination. There are hundreds of miles to this road and so much to unpack and discover. Sometimes the thought of how long this road goes on for is daunting, other times it's inspiring. Just like many other things in life, healing comes in waves. It ebbs and flows. But it's the most beautiful journey.

In the next few chapters, I share everything that I've learned along the way that has helped me to get to this beautiful, peaceful place that I am in now. I hope it helps you too.

There are fill-in sections in each chapter to help you get started on your healing work, but feel free to get a notebook and write more in depth. The notebook I kept in the first two years of my healing journey is sacred to me. Not only do I reference it now to help me navigate through difficult situations, but it is also a beautiful reminder of how much progress I've made and continue to make. Try writing everything down, you won't regret it!

Chapter 12

I Am Getting to Know Myself

THE FIRST THIRTY years of my life, I only knew myself on a surface level. I followed the rules, was a people pleaser, wanted to keep the peace, wanted to fit in and be accepted, wanted to be loved, and so on. As I've already mentioned, my self-identity and self-worth came from external sources—Parker's love for me, my success at work, whether my parents were proud of me, or how good of an aunt, friend, or sister I was. I only felt good about myself when I was making everyone around me feel good about themselves. I spent my life making sure everyone around me felt comfortable, seen, and loved only to wake up and realize that I had never made myself feel comfortable, seen, or loved.

I didn't want the next thirty years to look or feel like that. I had to figure out who I truly was. I had to get back to the basics and that's what I did. You can do it too.

Control the controllable. Everything feels dark and scary when you're going through something difficult. None of us know what the future holds (even psychics can only see so much), and it's normal to be scared of what comes next. Instead of focusing on the unknown, focus on what is in your control.

- Make a list of all the aspects of your life that are in your control (examples: daily routine, exercise, therapy or support groups, job, finances, thoughts, support from family and friends, your decisions, self-care routine, etc.). This will help lighten the heaviness, overwhelming thoughts, and anxiety. Making this list allows some light to shine through the darkness. This list is yours, and you can take comfort in knowing that no one can take it away from you.

- What aspects of your life are within your control?
  1. _____
  2. _____
  3. _____

- Write out your daily routine and do your best to stick to it. Routine is especially vital when there's a lot going on in your life. You can trust it. It feels comfortable and safe. It allows you to be in control of your time.

  What is your daily routine?

  Monday _____

  Tuesday _____

  Wednesday _____

  Thursday _____

  Friday _____

  Saturday _____

  Sunday _____

- Review your finances and bills. Money is a huge stressor, so mapping out a solid monthly plan takes the uncertainty out. It allows you to make informed financial decisions and be in control for the present and future.

Monthly Budget

Income
Net Monthly Income $ _____
Other Monthly Income $ _____
Total Monthly Income $ _____

Expenses
Mortgage/Rent $_____
Utilities $ _____
Car/Transportation $_____
Cell Phone $ _____
Food/Groceries $ _____
Debt/Loan Payments $_____
Misc. $ _____
Total Expenses $ _____

Subtract your total expenses from your monthly income and evaluate!

- If your expenses are more than your income or the same as your income, work on ways to cut expenses and/or consider working overtime to increase your income. Remember, everything is temporary, so you might not always have to cut expenses or work overtime, but in the meantime, we are working to get your finances in a balanced place.
- If your expenses are less than your income and you feel comfortable with your monthly finances, leave it be!
- Talk through worst-case scenarios and a solution for each with a family member, friend, or trained professional. This will quiet the negative, scary thoughts that play on a loop in your mind. You have a solution and plan for every scenario in front of you. You are in control.

Worst-case scenario #1 _____

_____

_____

_____

Solution #1 _____

_____

_____

_____

Worst-case scenario 2 _____

_____

_____

_____

Solution #2 _____

_____

_____

_____

Worst-case scenario #3 _____

_____

_____

_____

Solution #3 _____

_____

_____

_____

- Don't be afraid to ask for help and lean on the people in your life. You're not fighting this battle alone. Their insight and perspective can help calm your mind and help you start thinking about your next steps moving forward.

  Who can you trust and ask for help?

  1. _____
  2. _____
  3. _____

A calm, quiet mind allows you to begin to look within.

Get to know yourself. To get to know yourself on a soul level, you've got to dig deep. I'm talking real deep. No more surface-level shit. No more running from yourself.

- Every day, spend five minutes in front of a mirror and say something nice about yourself. (Examples: congratulate yourself on an accomplishment that day, compliment yourself, talk nicely to yourself.) I know this sounds weird and uncomfortable, but it changes the dialogue you have with yourself. You start to recognize the person staring back at you again. You become friends with yourself again. You become comfortable with yourself again

As you start to become more comfortable with yourself, you become less afraid to be alone with yourself and your thoughts. You enter a space within yourself that allows you to open up your body and mind to new things, new passions. One step at a time.

Write something nice about yourself!

1. _____

2. _____

3. _____

4. _____

5. _____

Spend time alone. When you eliminate the distractions, you have no choice but to sit with yourself and your thoughts. That's the place where you begin to dig deep.

- Try to spend thirty minutes a day alone. This could be your drive to work, taking a walk on your break, taking a bath or shower, meditating, sneaking into bed by yourself, etc.
- During those thirty minutes, ask yourself deep, tough questions.

What do you want to change and heal? _____

_____

_____

_____

_____

How is your heart today? _____

_____

_____

_____

_____

How was your day? _____

_____

_____

_____

_____

What were the good and bad parts of your day? _____

_____

_____

_____

How did you navigate through your emotions today?_____

_____

_____

_____

_____

What made you feel great today? _____

_____

_____

_____

_____

What happened today that you want to leave behind and not

bring forward into tomorrow? _____

_____

_____

_____

_____

- Those thirty minutes will grow to an hour or a day, and you'll start having real conversations with yourself. Before you know it, being alone will become a lovely place to be. You'll start trusting yourself and your judgment. You'll finally be comfortable being inside of that beautiful mind of yours because it's your home and no one can take it away from you. The stillness of yourself becomes your safe space. It's one of my favorite places to be, and I hope it becomes one of yours too.

Embrace your passions and try new things. Let's start by embracing (maybe re-embracing) some passions and hobbies you love (or loved in the past) and trying some new ones too.

- I believe one of the byproducts of being in a toxic situation, whether that be a relationship, marriage, or friendship, is losing sight of your passions. You spend so much time putting that person first, trying to make things better, and doing what they want to do that you lose your own piece of happiness in it. So let's make another list!

  What do/did you love to do? What brings you joy? What are you passionate about? What makes you excited? (Examples: reading, painting, hiking, yoga, dancing, swimming, watching movies, organizing, shopping, decorating.)
  1. _____
  2. _____
  3. _____
  4. _____
  5. _____

- Once you have your list, start by doing one of the things on your list once per week. Start slow because it can be overwhelming doing something again that you haven't done in a while. We want this exercise to make you feel excited, maybe a bit nervous, but not overwhelmed. As the weeks go on, start doing one to three items per week. Remember, we are prioritizing you, your passions, and your happiness.

- Once you've embraced your previous passions, let's add some new potential interests to the list. Is there something you've been wanting to try but haven't gotten around to? Is there a class you've been wanting to take, but you've been too nervous? It's the perfect time to get out of your comfort zone and try something new. Again, we don't want to try too many new things at once. We are starting off slow and simple by picking one thing. As time goes on and you get more comfortable being outside of your comfort zone, you can add more and more.

New potential interests

1. _____

2. _____

3. _____

By embracing old things for the first time in a while and trying new things, I showed myself I could do hard things. I could do things that initially made me really nervous. I could overcome my fears and make myself proud in doing so. Sometimes we just have to get out of our own way and trust that we are capable.

Don't be afraid to ask for help. I'm sure you're similar to me in seldomly asking for help, always believing you can push through, and having an "I can do this by myself" mentality. But guess what? Asking for help doesn't negate your strength or ability to do it all by yourself. You passed that test a long time ago. We know you're a badass. We know you can move that mountain by yourself. But you don't have to. You and I were never meant to face all of this alone.

The beautiful thing about asking for help or letting others be there for you is realizing it doesn't make you weak, needy, or a burden to others, as you thought. It makes you stronger, more remarkable, and powerful. So let's try it.

Who do you trust the most in your life? _____

Who brings you comfort? _____

Who understands you? _____

Put these people at the top of your list!

- Whether you have the conversation by text, phone, or Facetime, reach out to the person and express that you are having a tough day or going through a difficult situation and would love their advice and support. You want to lead with that so they know you're not in the best place, and they can respond intentionally. By responding intentionally, I mean they might be in a meeting and won't be able to talk until twelve. Or they might be driving and a phone call would be better than texting. Or maybe it's the perfect time for them and you can dive right in.

- Once you've established the timing for the conversation, allow yourself to be present and vulnerable. Let your guard down and express how you're feeling and what you're going through. If you need to cry, cry. Crying is so therapeutic and underrated. Listen to the advice you're being given and even write it down so you can go back to it.

- If you don't have someone in your life that you can trust or turn to, or if you've been thinking about speaking to a professional, I encourage you to try therapy. Finding the right therapist can be difficult and it takes time. It's kind of like dating—either there's a connection or there's not. If there's not, that doesn't mean you give up; it means you keep searching.

- Starting therapy is overwhelming, so take it one step at a time. Once you've found a therapist that you connect with, commit to one time a week for a month and then re-evaluate. Remember, everything is temporary. You don't have to be in therapy forever. You don't always have to go once a week.

- Talking to a certified, trained professional to help you heal, grow, and navigate through life is a game changer. Therapy allows you to peel back every layer of yourself and heal each one individually.

I know there are some people reading this that don't believe in therapy. I was you. As I mentioned earlier in the book, I was wildly against therapy before I got to rock bottom and had no other choice but to seek professional help. Having been on this journey for a few years now, it dawned on me that when you have a fever, you go to the doctor. When your back hurts, you go to the chiropractor. When your tooth aches, you go to the dentist. When your car breaks down, you bring it to the mechanic. So why are we so against seeking professional help for our mental health? We haven't learned the tools to navigate through heartbreak, divorce, anxiety, depression, job changes, people dying, and other huge life changes. We think we know all the answers, but we don't. We think we're strong enough to power through, but it's not about strength. Remember, we already passed the strength test. It's about growth. It's about not repeating the same cycles and patterns. It's about prioritizing your mental health.

Therapy has changed my life. It's one of the greatest decisions I ever made. I wouldn't be where I am today without it. I encourage you to give it a try.

The support of family, friends, mentors, professionals, and doctors is pivotal in your healing. If I could go back in time and change something, it would be to have asked for help sooner, to have leaned on my family and friends more, and to have started therapy earlier in life.

You are not alone.

What I've learned: Getting to know yourself and facing yourself is really fucking hard. It takes courage and grit. It's not for the faint of heart. We only have one life and it goes really quick. So let's choose ourselves and our healing. Let's do the hard work. Let's make the next thirty years way better than the last thirty years. At the end of the day, we only have ourselves. One body, one mind, one life. Let's make those a beautiful place to be. You deserve it. I believe in you, and I'm rooting for you!

Chapter 13

I Am Forgiving Myself

FORGIVENESS TAKES TIME. A lot of time and self-reflection. The funny thing about forgiveness is that it has so much more to do with you forgiving yourself than it does with the person who caused you pain. It's a weird concept to accept, but as you move through your healing journey, you realize it. Here are the steps that helped me to lean into forgiveness and set myself free.

Acknowledge the pain and hurt. To acknowledge the pain and hurt is to sit with it.

- Take time to acknowledge what you've been through and the pain it's caused you. Let go of the need to downplay, deflect, or suppress the pain. Let the pain be what it truly is. It's raw and uncomfortable. It can be as simple as "The day I found out Parker was cheating, a part of me died. I lost a piece of myself that day and it hurt like fucking hell."

What and who has caused you pain and how?

_____

_____

_____

_____

Your story is real. Your memories are real. Your feelings are real. Your pain is real.

Accept the things we cannot change. We have to accept the things we cannot change, because they don't deserve to hold power over us or our minds any longer than they already have.

- Let's make another list!

What are some things you wish you could change, but you can't? For me this looks like: I can't change what I've been through. I can't go back in time. I can't change what Parker did to me. I can't change how I chose to navigate through my toxic relationship. I can't change how long I stayed for. I can't change the fact that I didn't ask for help or start therapy earlier in life.

1. _____

2. _____

3. _____

When we are in acceptance and at peace, we can let go.

Commit to letting go. Letting go of the person that hurt you allows you to release them from your space, energy, and mind. It allows you to take your power back. It's time to cut the chains that are holding you back. You are worthy of living a life that is authentic, peaceful, and genuine, with no ties to your past holding you back.

- Close your eyes and imagine the person you want to release from your energy floating away in front of you. Visualize the person coming out of your body and energy and moving away from you. I know it sounds weird, but we want the universe to know that you no longer want that energy in your energy. They can take it. They can have it. You don't want it.

It's time to set yourself free!

Forgive yourself. We've acknowledged, accepted, and released. Now we have to forgive ourselves.

- Write a letter to yourself for all of the things you want to forgive yourself for. For me, I forgive myself for:
  - letting myself down for so long.
  - losing myself in that relationship.
  - all of the times I recognized how badly I was being treated and didn't leave.
  - accepting less than I deserve.
  - hurting so badly and not trying to get myself help sooner.
  - not telling my parents sooner.
  - putting everyone else first and myself last.
  - not realizing the magical, powerful, and badass energy within myself.

Dear Me,
I forgive myself for

_____

_____

_____

_____

_____

_____

_____

I promise that I will never put myself in a position where I compromise any parts of myself again.

Love, Me

What I've learned: You only have today. Life is too short to let your past determine your future. We have to face it, accept it, and let it go so we can do ourselves the biggest favor and forgive ourselves. In forgiving ourselves, we are putting our past to bed. We are at peace with it. This allows us to move freely into our new future, something we all deserve!

Chapter 14

I Am Accepting Myself

I SPENT A lot of time on the stretch of road that led to fully accepting myself. I spent months walking this road, and I still come back and revisit it. When you have very little sense of self, you are essentially starting from scratch, and that takes a lot of time and energy. So buckle up!

Here's my mini map:

1. Self-awareness
2. Self-care
3. Self-love
4. Self-worth
5. Self-acceptance

Self-awareness. Self-awareness is about seeing and understanding yourself clearly. You need to do a lot of deep inner reflection to understand what makes you you. I want you to be brutally honest with yourself without placing judgment on yourself. (This was *very* hard for me.)

- Let's make another list! Ask yourself what are your:
- o Weaknesses _____

_____

_____

- o Strengths _____
  _____
  _____

- o Flaws _____
  _____
  _____

- o Superpowers _____
  _____
  _____

- o Triggers_____
  _____
  _____

- o Positive Habits _____
  _____
  _____

- o Negative Habits _____
  _____
  _____

Establishing a deep understanding of self allows you to become more comfortable within yourself, have more confidence, better manage and regulate your emotions, and develop better communication and decision-making skills.

Self-awareness is key to a happier and healthier life.

Self-care. Maybe like me, you've gone a while without doing something nice for yourself. Self-care is so important because it enhances our well-being, decreases stress, increases our energy, and allows us to put ourselves first!

- Create a feel-good list.
  What are things you can do for yourself that make you feel good? For me, this was taking a bath with Epsom salt, doing my skin

care routine, getting a massage, going to hot yoga, sitting in the sun, painting, or going for walks.

1. _____

2. _____

3. _____

4. _____

5. _____

- Start by carving out three days a week to do one of the things on your feel-good list!

  Once you start prioritizing your self-care, you will see how much it helps to improve your mental, physical, and emotional well-being. It won't be long before you see the benefits and how recharged you feel. Naturally, your feel-good list will grow and so will the amount of time you dedicate to self-care. It's a beautiful progression and your mind, body, and soul will thank you!

Self-love. Self-love started in the mirror a few chapters ago, but there's so much more to it! Self-love is an appreciation of oneself and having a high regard for your happiness. Here's how to cultivate self-love:

- Speak nicely to and about yourself whether you are alone or having a conversation with someone else. When negative thoughts and criticism sneak up on you, kill them with kindness. Counteract the negative thought with a positive action and thought.

  For example:

  Negative thought: "My face looks puffy today."

  Positive action: I can ice roll my face for twenty minutes. Then I can put on makeup that will make me feel snatched and beautiful.

Positive thought: "My skin is clear!"
Try it!

Negative thought   _____

Positive action   _____

Positive thought   _____

Negative thought   _____

Positive action   _____

Positive thought   _____

- Take care of and nourish your body. Revisit the previous section of self-care for action items from your feel-good list that will help you to do this.

- Stop comparing yourself to other people. I know all too well how difficult this is in the world we live in. Every time you open social media, you see a beautiful, perfectly filtered and edited person. But that's just it—it's not real. Social media is a highlight reel. I encourage you to take a look at the accounts you follow on social media and think about the effect their content has on you. If they don't make you feel good, motivate you, or inspire you, consider unfollowing them.

- Surround yourself with people who make you feel your best. We are only accepting authentic, genuine connections and energy from others. You want to feel like your cup is filled to the brim with happiness, love, inspiration, and deep connection when you leave the people in your life. If you feel drained after being with certain people, spend less time with them or cut off access to your energy entirely.

Practicing self-love allows us to prioritize ourselves and our mental, emotional, and physical well-being. *You* are the most important person in your life!

Self-worth. Self-worth is that power and force within you that breeds the confident energy that you share with the world and yourself.

Let's imagine we are building you out of bricks. The first brick is self-awareness. Right on top of that is self-care, third is self-love, and suddenly we have a solid structure that has grown quite tall. We've spent a lot of time and energy building from the ground up. We can now look back on our hard work and be proud.

- Ask yourself:
  - What have you achieved that makes you feel proud of yourself? (For me, this is writing and publishing this book to share my story and help others.) _____

  _____

  _____

  - What do you respect about yourself? (For me, this is my ability to say no to the things that no longer align with me.)

  _____

  _____

  _____

  - What do you love about yourself? (For me, I love how resilient I am. I know I am strong enough to handle anything that is thrown my way.) _____

  _____

  _____

  - What do you value about yourself? (For me, I value my heart. After everything I've been through, I never allowed my heart to harden. I continue to pour love out of me and accept love in.) _____

_____

_____

Self-worth comes in time. This structure you've built is beautiful from the inside out and holds so much value. It is worthy of the space it holds and doesn't need the validation of anyone else. It's a masterpiece. You are a masterpiece.

Self-acceptance. Self-acceptance is the ability to accept all facets of ourselves—the good, valuable, positive, negative, less desirable, etc. It's a state of being in acceptance of everything that makes you you.

Every stop along this road has helped us to reach the exit of self-acceptance. If you can answer the following questions with a "yes," then you are truly in acceptance of yourself. If some of your answers are "maybe" or "no," I would work through the mini map again, starting at self-awareness. Self-acceptance is a long road and it takes patience and time.

Do you accept yourself without conditions?

☐ Yes ☐ No ☐ Maybe

Do you embrace everything that makes you you?

☐ Yes ☐ No ☐ Maybe

Do you feel a true sense of belonging within yourself?

☐ Yes ☐ No ☐ Maybe

Do you feel whole and complete within yourself?

☐ Yes ☐ No ☐ Maybe

Are you living for you and only you?

☐ Yes ☐ No ☐ Maybe

Do you trust yourself?

☐ Yes ☐ No ☐ Maybe

Self-acceptance is one of the greatest, most powerful gifts you can ever work towards and give yourself.

Chapter 15

I Am Protecting Myself

PROTECTING MYSELF AND my energy is one of the most important things that I've learned to do in my healing journey.

Set boundaries. Before starting my healing journey, I had no boundaries. If I'm being honest, I didn't even know what boundaries were. This was abundantly clear in my relationship with Parker. When I started my healing journey, I learned about boundaries through therapy, and I started to practice setting them in my life. As a recovering people pleaser, this was not easy to do, but with a lot of practice, I am now a great boundary setter. And you can be too!

- Practice saying no. You are your main priority, and you have to do what's best for you. If you don't feel like doing something, don't feel the need to overexert yourself to make other people happy. Be honest about how you are feeling and decline the invitation.
- Don't be afraid to speak what's on your mind. If you are worried about how the people around you might respond, you are not surrounding yourself with the right people. When you express what you're feeling or thinking, the right people will meet you with a response that is respectful and supportive.
- Release and let go of the people, places, and things that no longer align with you. If something or someone is not an energetic match, let's practice removing them from our energy and space.

When people show you who they are, believe them the first time. People can only meet you as far as they've met themselves, so if someone is falling short of your expectations, it's not your mission to help them get there. It's your job to release them because they aren't an energetic match.

- Practice not looking past things and not giving people the benefit of the doubt. We have to stop spinning the narrative in our mind that turns people into who we want them to be. People are who they are, and we can't change them.

Start evaluating. I know you're probably thinking... evaluations? Hear me out!

Daily evaluations are internal and they allow you to check in with yourself.

- Ask yourself: How are you? How are you feeling? How did you sleep? Where are you mentally?
  Action: If your internal gas tank is empty: You need to show yourself a lot of grace. Make a conscious effort to not push yourself too hard and to up your self-care practices. Give yourself extra time for everything so you don't bring on more anxiety than you already have. If your internal gas tank is full: You can extend yourself further. You will feel confident in your goals because you're on your game. You can create new goals because you're fully charged and thinking clearly.

Quarterly evaluations are external and allow you to check in on your relationships and surroundings.
- Ask yourself: Are the people you are surrounding yourself with an energetic match? Are you happy at your job? Is your self-care routine working? Does your exercise routine make you feel good? Have you tried something new?

Action: Depending on your answers to each of those questions, come up with a plan of action for the next three months. Some things will stay exactly the same and other things will completely change. Nonetheless, give yourself the time and space to evaluate, plan, and make changes. Prioritize yourself so you can make the next three months better than the last three months.

By setting clear boundaries, you are making a promise to yourself to...

Honor your standards.
Be treated how you deserve to be treated.
Allow people to meet you where you've met yourself.
Set high expectations for yourself and the people in your life.
Never settle again.
Value quality over quantity.
Only allow people in your life who have earned their spot.

Chapter 16

I Am in Alignment

THE STRETCH OF road in my healing journey that is alignment has been one of my favorite parts. It's the place where I started to see the results of my hard work.

Alignment within yourself. You have done and will continue to do the hard work on yourself and your healing that will bring you into alignment. Alignment within yourself is the result of living your best life, trusting yourself, and showing up as the person you know you are meant to be.

If you are on the same energetic wavelength as the following statements, you are in alignment or you are in the process of getting there.

I am exactly where I'm supposed to be.

I am not worried or concerned about what comes next.

I am showing up as my raw, authentic self.

I trust myself and my decisions.

I am unapologetically speaking my truth.

I am setting healthy boundaries.

I am no longer comparing myself to others.

I have so much gratitude for my journey, the universe, and myself.

Being in alignment with yourself puts you in a high energetic frequency that allows more beautiful blessings to pour in from the universe. It's a magical place to be!

Alignment with the universe. The universe knows when you are in alignment with yourself and you've put in the hard work, and it wants to reward you! So how do you redeem those rewards? Here are a few ways:

- What you speak out into the universe comes back tenfold, so be sure to keep your thoughts, wishes, and dreams positive and uplifting.
- When you wake up every morning, practice saying out loud, "Universe, show me how good it can get."
- When you ask the universe for something, put yourself in the mindset and energetic frequency of already having it. Let's say you want a new car. Normally, you'd say "Universe, I want a new car. I've had my car for ten years now and I need a new car." I challenge you to change it to "I've purchased my brand-new car. I am so grateful to have found the exact car I wanted. I love the way it drives. I am so incredibly thankful for my new car." This is manifestation at its finest and it works. Try it!

Embrace change. We've worked super hard to get to a place where we know ourselves, we are confident in ourselves, and we trust ourselves. So let's push that even further and trust that no matter what comes our way, we are strong enough to handle it.

Change is inevitable. Your goal is to work towards finding such a peaceful and balanced place within yourself (through the steps we've already taken in Part 2) that nothing can shake you.

Try practicing this exercise when the fear of change kicks in:

- It's normal to be scared of change, the future, and the unknown. That initial feeling of being scared is natural. Sit with that feeling for a few minutes, then change your inner thoughts to "I am strong enough to make it through anything. I am capable of embracing change. I can handle anything. No matter what, I will be okay!"

You have the tools within yourself to not only face change but to embrace and conquer it. I believe in you!

Seek deeper connections. We started evaluating our connections in the "I am protecting myself" chapter, so let's take it one step further.

- Ask yourself if the people in your life love and understand you on a soul level. If the answer is yes, keep those people close to you and allocate the most time to them. If the answer is no, invest less of your energy into these people.
- Ask yourself how you feel when you are around the people in your life? If you feel fulfilled, inspired, motivated, loved, and cared for, keep those people close to you and allocate the most time to them. If you feel drained, tired, overwhelmed, insecure, upset, uneasy, etc., move your energy away from these people.
- Ask the people in your life the following questions to get to know them on a deeper level:
  o What makes you excited to get out of bed in the morning?
  o What keeps you up at night?
  o Where do you see yourself in five years?
  o How has your childhood impacted you as an adult?
  o What are your dreams and goals?
  o What is your biggest fear?
  o What have you been through and how did it change you?

As you come into alignment within yourself, you will attract and keep the right people in your life. And the right people will stay, they will love you, and they will take care of you and your heart. We are releasing unfulfilling, surface-level connections because we deserve better.

Chapter 13

I Am the Best Version of Myself

AND WE'VE REACHED the final stretch of road that is our healing journey. It's the place where all we've been working through, working towards, practicing, and writing down falls into place. It's a place where we can look back and reflect on the incredible progress we've made and the mountains we've moved.

Something to keep in mind: Yes, we've done the deep inner work and that will keep us at peace and balanced within ourselves no matter what is thrown our way, but not every day is going to be rainbows and butterflies. On the days when it *is* rainbows and butterflies, soak it all in and express gratitude towards yourself and the universe. On the harder days, show yourself grace and remember that everything is temporary.

What does it feel like to be the best version of yourself?

You are living authentically.

You are living a life that is true to *you*!

You continue to do the healing work because our healing is never complete. We are all a work in progress.

You feel whole within yourself.

You are living a life that is a reflection of your personality, heart, spirit, mind, and soul.

You lead your life with intention and integrity.

You believe in yourself.

You believe you can have it all and no one is going to stop you.

You have everything you need within yourself.

You recognize, acknowledge, and celebrate the power and magic within yourself.

You are worthy of the space you hold in a room.

You are confident in yourself and what you bring to the table.

You believe you have the qualities and tools within yourself to make your wildest dreams and goals come true.

If you had to bet on one person, you'd bet on yourself. Without hesitation and without doubt, you'd bet on yourself.

What does it look like to be the best version of yourself?

I want you to close your eyes. I want you to imagine yourself standing in front of you. I want you to imagine a beautiful yellow beam of light shining out of the core of your body. It's radiant like the sun. It's pure and gentle. It's strong and powerful. It's magical and magnetic.

That yellow beam of light is all of the beautiful things that make you you. It's the healing you've done. It's the pain and trauma you've overcome. It's the way you've grown to love and accept yourself. It's the boundaries you've set. It's the way you've let go of the things that no longer align with you. It's the alignment you've found within yourself and the universe.

That yellow beam of light does not dim to fit in or make others feel comfortable. It's an honor to stand in your light. It continuously shines brightly as you share the greatest version of yourself with the world. That yellow beam of light is irrevocably yours, and no one can take it from you ever again.

• • •

If you'd asked me two and a half years ago if I thought I could get to the place I am now, I would have said no way. I had no idea what the future held. The only thing I knew was that I couldn't stay the same. I couldn't stay in the same place I'd been.

My comeback was personal. I was doing this for the girl who so badly wanted to be loved by a man that could never love her the way she deserved. I was doing this for the girl who thought she had to carry the weight of the world on her shoulders to protect a man that never deserved it. I was doing this for all of the nights I lay in bed alone and cried myself to sleep. I was doing this for the girl who put on a brave face at her wedding so everyone else could be happy. I was doing this for the girl who couldn't say one nice thing to describe herself. I was doing this for the girl who never felt like she was enough. I was doing this for me.

Every day that I woke up and chose myself, my yellow beam of light shined a little brighter. As I type these words on this page, my yellow beam of light is the brightest it's ever been. My yellow beam of light is everything I am and everything I've overcome. It's not settling in love until I meet the person who is deserving of my go-to-the-end-of-the-earth type of love. It's protecting my energy, peace, and space. It's my healing journey. It's sharing my psychic gifts with the world. It's sleeping peacefully at night. It's writing and publishing this book. It's everything that makes me Marissa, and I'm never going to lose myself or my light again.

My healing, without a shadow of a doubt, is the greatest gift I've ever given myself. It's the hardest work I've ever done, but I would do it a million times over to be in the exact place I am now. A place where I am the best version of myself. The greatest version of myself.

Chapter 13

I Am You

I KNOW I'M not the only one. I know there are other people walking this earth that have loved so incredibly hard and lost themselves in their relationship or marriage. I know others have been betrayed by someone they loved, and they were scared to leave. I feel so deeply in my soul for you and your journey because I know firsthand how hard it is. I am you.

I learned the hard way that you don't get a reward for how much you can endure at the hands of another person. You just lose yourself entirely. Maybe you're still in the relationship or marriage. Maybe you're still fighting the not-so-good fight. Maybe your friends and family have told you to leave. Maybe you've tried leaving and it never works. Maybe they're your financial stability. Maybe you have children together. Maybe you feel like you'll never find love again. Maybe you feel like you have no other choice. I am you.

Your go-to-the-end-of-the-earth kind of love isn't for everyone, and most are not deserving of it. I know you thought your love could carry them through their darkness and demons, but the unhealed parts of them are not yours to mend or carry. You have to set it down. It's too heavy. I know you're scared of change and what comes next, but you have to trust me. I am you.

On the other side of your fear is something that is unmatched. It's something that money can't buy. It's something that another person can't bring you. It's you choosing yourself and finding yourself again. It's you healing the deepest parts of yourself. It's you forgiving yourself. It's you accepting yourself. It's you protecting yourself. It's you finding alignment within yourself. And last but not least, it's you becoming the greatest version of yourself. I am you.

Above all else, I want you to know that you are not alone. You are strong. You are intelligent. You are beautiful. You are resilient. You are powerful. You are capable. You are perfect. You are enough. You are not playing small anymore. You are a force to be reckoned with. You will change the world. And I'm so fucking proud of you. I am you and you are me.

Acknowledgements

THE AMOUNT OF gratitude I have for my family, friends, and therapist is immeasurable. Thank you from the bottom of my heart.

My sister, Victoria—My secret keeper and my first phone call every time. You walked hand in hand with me through the darkness and never left my side. There will never be enough words or ways to thank you. I'm so grateful to be in this new chapter of healing, growth, and celebration with you right next to me. To-the-end-of-the-earth kind of love, till-the-end-of-time kind of bond. I love you with everything I am!

My mom—You are everything to me. Your unconditional love, support, and guidance pulled me through. I'm sorry for not telling you sooner, but I couldn't bear to see you hurt as much as I was hurting because we both know you would have. You are the world's best mother, and I'm so lucky you are mine. I love you so much!

My dad—You are the greatest example of a dad and husband. Your "We'll figure it out, Mariss" is what got me through. The next man in my life is going to be just like you. A protector, provider, and one that makes me feel safe. I love you more than you'll ever know!

My brother, Edward John—You gave me the tough love I needed, and I love you for that! No one makes me laugh harder, and I will forever need your jokes. I look forward to the day you turn this book into a Lifetime movie. I love you!

My brother-in-law, Kraig—Thank you for standing up and speaking up for me. Thank you for protecting me. Thank you for making me laugh uncontrollably through my bad and good days. I love you. Say it back!

My sister-in-law, Stephanie—Thank you for your support, love, and guidance. I'm so grateful to have you in my life. I love you!

My nieces and nephews, Hadley, Eddie, Kolton, and Max—You guys are too young to know this, but you were the sunshine in my life when everything else felt gray. The kisses, belly laughs, hugs, and smiles pulled me through. Being your aunt is one of my greatest blessings, and I promise to always say yes when Mom and Dad say no. Pinky promise. I love you!

Aunt Renee and Uncle Chris—Some of my fondest memories are sitting on your couch for months while you guys helped me walk through my toughest days. I wouldn't be where I am in my healing journey if it wasn't for you two. Thank you. I love you!

My best friend, Katy—My twin soul. I know I will never walk a day in this life alone because I've got you. I am forever grateful. You are the greatest friend anyone could ever ask for. Thank you for believing in me and all my crazy dreams. I love you!

My best friend, Danielle—The last two years have been a whirlwind to say the least, but we've been each other's strength every step of the way. We can make it through anything together. I am so grateful for our friendship. Thank you for sharing your guardian angel with me. I know we are and will continue to make him proud. I love you!

My therapist, Rachel—You changed my life. You walked through the darkness with me even when I couldn't see the light. Now that I am standing in the light, I want to thank you. You brought me back to myself, the greatest gift I've ever been given. You are remarkable, and you're changing the world one person at a time. I love you!

Made in United States
North Haven, CT
12 July 2024

54738944R00078